MAGIK OF LAKSHMI

David Thompson

MAGIK OF LAKSHMI

David Thompson

For Lakshmi & Kali

A Hindu is interested in the welfare of all: not merely humans, but all living beings.
~Yogi Adityanath

A Legal Disclaimer:

By Law, I am obliged to let you know that this is for entertainment purposes only, and does not claim to prevent or cure any diseases. The advice in this book should not be construed as financial, medical, or psychological advice. Please seek such advice from a professional.

By purchasing this book, and working the rituals, you understand that results are not guaranteed. In light of this and in the unlikely event that the material in this book does not work for you or, in the very unlikely event, this book causes physical harm to you or a loved one, you agree that you will not hold David Thompson, our affiliates and employees liable for any damages you may experience or incur.

Each individual's success depends on his or her background, dedication, desire, and motivation.

A Warning:

This is very powerful material. When worked properly, you may see unexpected results. These rituals and petitions are like electricity, the energy will flow in the direction of the intended output. In saying this, please be firm in your intentions and make absolutely sure what you want is truly what you desire.

As they say, be careful what you wish for, you just might get it.

Hello!

For you, this might be the first book on magik, or the first book on MY magik you are reading. I strive to make this as accessible as possible for people new to Magik.

Many readers may not know this, but I do not tend to "blow my own horn," so I don't market my services like I should. On the advice of multiple people, I'm including this brief "horn blowing" in all new books.

I have a modest website: https://davepsychic.com

Everyone sometimes has trouble making their magik work. To that, I offer ritual services, I also do readings and attunements, and I'm considering some protection, removal services. Most dark/black entities are connected to larger black systems, and it can take a bit to cast them away.

I also offer one-on-one workings, which is an educational program. I can teach you based upon your level, and I expect you to actually take part in the exercises.

Check it out. I also have a contact page, but it might take me a few days to answer due to the volume of emails I get daily.

INTRODUCTION

As with Sorath, I first "met" Lakshmi while writing my Furies books. She played a major role in the backstory, which helped clarify the main character's ability to see the usually invisible Furies.

I followed a book by Baal Kadmon and used the time-honored invocation—repeating her mantra 108 times.

108 times.

Phew.

But why 108?

In Hindu magik, sound is a direct link to divine energy. Mantras align you with the deity through vibration. The number 108 holds deep cosmic meaning. In Vedic cosmology, the Sun's diameter is about 108 times that of Earth, and the distance between them is the same ratio—symbolizing universal harmony. In yogic systems, 108 energy lines (nadis) converge at the heart chakra. That number opens the divine flow.

Mantras aren't just words. They're vibrational keys. Repeating a mantra 108 times builds resonance. It draws the deity's presence closer. That's why mala beads—usually with 108 beads—are used to keep count and sharpen focus. Each repetition strengthens the bridge between material and spirit.

Lakshmi's energy, when it came, was calm. Soothing. Not overwhelming, like Kali or Lilith. In my first invocation, she barely made herself known. But over time, her presence deepened. She just doesn't push through with the force some deities do. But her magik? Just as strong.

She also responds beyond the traditional mantra. I've used a redesigned Yantra—those sacred geometric diagrams from Tantric traditions—and included both my version and the classical one in this book. That gives you a solid baseline to work from in my magikal system.

If this is your first step into working with Hindu deities, you won't have to deal with the hiccups I had. Kali was my first. I sat down, chanted her mantra 108 times, lost count, and had to start over. Frustrating. I ended up making my own mala from string and wooden beads from a hobby shop. Crude—but it worked.

My exploration of Hindu deities didn't begin with Lakshmi. Back in the late '90s, many around me worked with Ganesha. I even had a small incense burner shaped like him.

But I didn't actively work with him until 2016, after trying a method from one of Baal Kadmon's books. That opened things up. Then came Kali. Also, through Baal's work.

Lakshmi didn't enter my magikal work until much later. Long after I wrote her into my Furies series. Only then did I invoke her. At first with the mantra. Later, through easier access methods that I developed.

Let's get going, shall we?

My Magik System

If you've read my other books, you can probably skip this section. But if you're new to my work, here's the short version of how I approach magik.

First off — "High Magik" wasn't a label I gave myself. I just called it magik. But others started calling it High Magik, so... blame them.

Out of curiosity, I once asked a random AI to define it. The response?

"High magick, also known as ceremonial magic or ritual magic, is a diverse set of rituals and practices that involve ceremony and accessories."

Fair enough. Most definitions center around rituals, accessories, summoning spirits—be they deities or daemons. Some people lump it in with Wicca or witchcraft. There are similarities, but they're not the same thing.

Now, my system?

I throw most of that out the window.

I play fast and loose with definitions. I simplify rituals. A lot.

Most traditional rituals are buried under layers of symbolism and outdated cultural habits. Sure, some of that has power. But you don't always need it to make contact with a spirit.

Especially with someone like Lakshmi.

She doesn't demand elaborate rites. She responds to clear intention, sincere desire, and a basic understanding of who she is and what she brings.

Ritual is a tool. Nothing more. It focuses energy. Sharpens your mind. Gets you into the right state. But it's not the source of power. That comes from alignment—of intent, of energy, of respect.

If you've got that? You're already halfway there.

Lakshmi Isn't Just About Money

Most people think Lakshmi is just the goddess of money. They're not wrong—but they're not right either. That's only one part of what she does. She's not a coin dispenser. You're not going to find her lurking behind an ATM, handing out stacks of money. She's the force behind all abundance. Wealth, yes—but also opportunity, timing, influence, clarity, power, luck, wisdom, and even love.

Lakshmi governs flow. When her energy is present,

things open up. Roads clear. People notice you. You get traction in areas that were stuck before. Money is just one way that energy shows itself. The deeper current is about prosperity in every direction.

To work with her properly, you need to understand how wealth actually functions. It's not isolated. It's not just about more cash. Prosperity moves through a larger system—shaped by fate, action, mindset, and energetic alignment. If someone's out of sync with that system, calling on Lakshmi won't fix anything. She doesn't respond to noise. She responds to signal. Intention, focus, clarity.

Western ceremonial magik leans toward control—summon, command, direct. Hindu magik doesn't work like that. It's not about forcing the divine. It's about aligning with it. Lakshmi's energy isn't yanked down. It's invited. It flows where it's honored. You don't "make" her show up—you become the kind of person she flows toward.

And that energy doesn't override karma. Past actions matter. If someone's been reckless, greedy, self-sabotaging—they've created resistance. That has to be cleared. Lakshmi doesn't wipe away consequences. She shows you how to shift them. She won't reward fear or scarcity. But she will amplify confidence, grace, and aligned effort.

One of the biggest mistakes people make is approaching her from a place of desperation. Neediness repels her. Begging shuts the door. Her presence is high, refined, steady. She comes where there's composure, worthiness, and intention. If you're clinging to money, hoarding wealth, or terrified of losing it—you're not in her current. You're blocking it.

This is where her other side shows up. Where there's Lakshmi, there's also Alakshmi. Same force—different motion. Lakshmi is wealth in flow. Alakshmi is wealth in collapse. Misused, feared, or corrupted wealth draws Alakshmi. She's not a villain. She's balance. Where one rules abundance, the other rules misfortune. The energy doesn't disappear—it just shifts form. That's why unethical wealth vanishes fast. The current corrects itself.

Lakshmi doesn't reward greed. She rewards stewardship. She's not about hoarding. She's about movement. Circulation. Energy that moves creates more energy. That's the secret. That's what most people miss.

Real wealth isn't just what you get. It's what you become. Lakshmi aligns you with that. She doesn't drop riches from the sky—she shifts your reality so that wealth becomes natural. Opportunities show up. The right people cross your path. You start winning, and it doesn't feel like luck. It feels right.

Working with her isn't about scripting long rituals or burning the perfect incense. It's about stepping into that frequency—matching her flow. She's not summoned. She's mirrored. Her current flows through those who already act like they belong in it.

This book isn't a guide to temporary gains. It's about lasting change. Lakshmi doesn't deal in quick fixes. She moves deep. She adjusts fate. She reshapes probability around you—but only if you're ready to meet her there.

Don't ask her to fix your life. Become someone fortune naturally favors.

That's her magik.

Lakshmi in My Magikal System

Magik is connection. That's the core of it. Aligning your energy with the forces that move the universe. You're not begging. You're not hoping. You're linking up with power. Genuine power.

In my work, spirits aren't far-off unknowables. They're not hidden behind temples or trapped in books. They're forces. They respond to intent, clarity, and direct contact. Lakshmi is one of the most responsive spirits I've ever worked with. She doesn't play games. She doesn't make you jump through hoops. Call her with sincerity, and she shows up. Fast.

Unlike some spirits—who make you crawl through years of devotion or layered initiations—Lakshmi comes when the connection is clean. Strong presence. Clear messages. You don't have to decode riddles or sift through dream fragments. She speaks in full sentences. Her energy is radiant, sure, but never overwhelming. She meets you where you are, provided you're showing up with respect and purpose.

That's why I simplify rituals. Complexity gets in the way. In traditional systems—especially deep-rooted ones like Hinduism—ritual often carries social, religious, and cultural weight. Offer this flower, wear that color, recite verses word-perfect in Sanskrit. That's fine. But none of it is required to connect.

I don't toss tradition out the window. But I strip it down. I keep what works and drop what doesn't. Spirits aren't judging your pronunciation. They don't need three bowls of rice, two bells, and a silk cloth to know you're serious. They read your energy. They feel your intent. And if your signal is strong? That's all that matters.

When I first contacted Lakshmi, I didn't do anything fancy. No shrine. No temple garland. Just a clear space, a strong call, and open energy. Her response was immediate. No fog. No static. Just a sense of presence so strong I could feel it in my skin. And she spoke. Not in riddles. In direct, practical words.

That's a pattern I've noticed with spirits of wealth and movement. They don't meander. They don't mystify. They act. Their energy is fast, focused, and unapologetic. Lakshmi carries that exact frequency. She brings flow. She clears blockages. She amplifies what's already moving.

Her current is abundance in every form—mental clarity, emotional peace, spiritual alignment, financial gain. But you can't force it. You have to open to it. If you're blocked—clinging to fear, stuck in scarcity, or dragging baggage—she'll let you know. She won't force change on you. But once you're ready? She flows like a river.

That's why my approach to Lakshmi magik is all about alignment, not theatrics. A single candle, a spoken invocation, and a clear intent is enough. If your focus is sharp and your energy's clean, that's more powerful than a full-scale puja done out of obligation or half-belief.

I work with spirits practically. My magik is direct. I test, tweak, strip down, and rebuild until it works clean every time. That's the system. It's not about ancient formulas. It's about energy transmission. Real contact. Real results. You'll see that across every part of this book.

I don't disrespect tradition. A lot of it works. A lot of it carries serious weight. But I shape it into something usable. Something that fits the way people actually work today. If a spirit doesn't care whether you're standing in a temple or your kitchen, why should your ritual pretend otherwise?

Lakshmi doesn't need drama. She needs clarity. She's

one of the best spirits to work with if you want to see fast, measurable change. When you call her properly, she responds. When you align, she moves. She doesn't make you guess. She shows up, and she flows through everything—money, love, timing, fate.

That's her power.

And in the pages ahead, I'll show you how to work with her using methods that are real, modern, and effective—without losing what makes her ancient and powerful.

CHAPTER 1

Hinduism's Polytheism & Pantheon

Hinduism is often called polytheistic, but this label barely scratches the surface of its theological complexity. Unlike the polytheism of the Greeks or the Norse, where gods were distinct individuals with their own spheres of influence, Hindu deities are facets of a greater divine energy. They are not separate beings in competition with each other, nor are they limited to a single function. Instead, they are expressions of an infinite cosmic force, different faces of the same divine reality. This is where the concept of polytheism in Hinduism diverges from the Western understanding. The gods and goddesses of the Hindu pantheon are manifestations—avatars, aspects, or energetic vibrations—of a singular, unfathomable consciousness.

At the heart of this system is Brahman, the ultimate, formless divine presence that pervades everything. Brahman is beyond comprehension, beyond gender, beyond all qualities that the human mind can grasp. The gods are the many ways this energy expresses itself within the material and spiritual planes, making it accessible to those who seek connection. Every deity is an aspect of Brahman, formed by the needs and consciousness of those who worship. When one calls upon Lakshmi, they are not summoning a separate goddess detached from all else. They are engaging with the principle of abundance itself, a conscious and active force of wealth, fortune, and prosperity. When one prays to Shiva, they are connecting with destruction and transformation as a living, divine current. These aren't separate entities in the way a Greek might have worshipped Apollo instead of Dionysus—these are faces of the same divine totality, each tuned to a different frequency of existence.

This perspective explains why Hindu gods have so many forms and avatars. Vishnu manifests as Rama, as Krishna, as Narasimha, each suited to a different era and purpose. Shiva takes on forms ranging from the cosmic dancer Nataraja to the fierce and ascetic Mahayogi. Even the goddesses—who are often mistakenly thought of as distinct figures—are part of the same divine energy. Lakshmi, Parvati, Durga, and Kali are not separate in essence but different aspects of Shakti, the primordial feminine force that moves all creation. Shakti itself is not separate from Brahman; it is Brahman in motion, the kinetic energy of the universe shaping itself into myriad forms.

This understanding of divine energy resolves the contradictions that seem to arise in Hindu mythology. A deity can be both benevolent and destructive, both loving and terrifying, because they are not limited to human moral structures. Vishnu, the preserver, can take on the ruthless form of Kalki, the destroyer of corruption, without ceasing to be Vishnu. Kali, the terrifying goddess of death, is also the deeply compassionate mother who protects her devotees. These contradictions only exist when viewed through the lens of Western dualism, which separates good from evil, creation from destruction. Hinduism acknowledges that all these forces emerge from the same source, and their divine embodiments simply shift according to the needs of the moment.

This is why worship in Hinduism is so fluid. A devotee may call upon different gods at different times without any contradiction. A merchant seeking prosperity may invoke Lakshmi, but when facing obstacles, they turn to Ganesha. A warrior might worship Durga for her fierce protection, then later seek Shiva for wisdom. This isn't inconsistency—it is an understanding that divinity is multi-faceted. The gods are not jealous, nor do they demand exclusive worship. They are energy, responding to the needs of those who call upon them.

The concept of Ishta Devata—one's chosen deity—further emphasizes this. Devotees may choose a specific god or goddess as their primary focus, not because that deity is the only truth, but because it is the form of divine energy that resonates most with them. Some are drawn to Krishna's playful, loving energy, others to Shiva's detached asceticism. Some find solace in Kali's ferocity, while others turn to Saraswati's wisdom. None of these choices invalidate the others. Each is a pathway into the divine, tailored to the individual's spiritual frequency.

The pantheon itself is an evolving, living thing. Deities merge, shift, and change over time. Some gods, like Indra, once held supreme positions and later faded into lesser roles. Others, like Vishnu and Shiva, grew in prominence as their aspects resonated with broader human experiences. New forms emerge as cultures shift, but the core truth remains the same: these are not separate entities in the way Western religion conceptualizes divine figures. They are focal points of energy, lenses through which humanity can access the unfathomable.

Even the stories of these deities reflect this fluidity. Myths about the gods are not static histories but living allegories. A story of Vishnu in one era may shift in another, adapting to the consciousness of the people who tell it. This is because the gods themselves are not limited to one identity. They are not bound by a single mythology or a fixed form. Their essence is universal, but their appearances and stories morph according to the needs of time and place. This is why Lakshmi can appear in different forms, from the gentle consort of Vishnu to an independent force of prosperity in tantric traditions. It is why Shiva can be a wild ascetic, a cosmic dancer, or a householder with a family. These are not contradictions—they are expansions of divine reality.

This approach to divinity is what allows Hinduism to accommodate an immense variety of traditions without conflict. Monotheistic traditions often struggle with variations in doctrine because their concept of deity is rigid, singular, and exclusive. In contrast, Hinduism acknowledges that divinity is too vast for a single path. Some traditions within Hinduism lean toward pure non-dualism, where all forms dissolve into Brahman. Others embrace the gods in a more personal way, forming deep relationships with specific deities. Both perspectives are valid because both emerge from the same source.

This understanding also transforms the way rituals function. When one makes offerings to a deity, they are not appeasing an external god in the way ancient Greek or Roman worshippers might have. They are aligning themselves with a particular frequency of divine energy. A Lakshmi puja is not just about seeking wealth—it is about attuning oneself to the vibration of abundance. A Shiva ritual is not simply about asking for protection or wisdom—it is about merging with the force of destruction and rebirth. The gods are not external figures granting favors; they are energies that, when invoked properly, bring the devotee into alignment with their essence.

This is why Hinduism, despite its immense variety of gods, remains fundamentally unified. The deities may appear countless, their stories vast and complex, but they all stem from the same source. They are waves upon the ocean of

Brahman, expressions of an infinite presence that is beyond name, beyond form, beyond comprehension. The gods are the pathways, but the ultimate reality remains unchanged. Whether one approaches through Lakshmi's grace, Shiva's detachment, Vishnu's compassion, or Kali's ferocity, they are all reaching toward the same divine truth.

Gods & Their Incarnations

Hindu theology does not see deities as fixed beings with singular identities. Instead, gods and goddesses take on multiple forms, each suited to a particular time, place, or cosmic need. These forms, known as avatars, allow divine energy to manifest in ways that humans can interact with more directly. Unlike the Western idea of reincarnation, which implies a cycle of birth and rebirth tied to karma, avatars are deliberate descents of divinity into the world. They are not bound by karma but arrive with purpose—to restore balance, guide humanity, or protect cosmic order. The concept of avatars is most famously associated with Vishnu, who takes on forms such as Rama and Krishna, but the goddesses also manifest in multiple incarnations. Lakshmi, the embodiment of wealth, fortune, and abundance, appears throughout Hindu mythology in various forms, each carrying a distinct aspect of her power.

Lakshmi's primary identity is that of the goddess of prosperity and the divine consort of Vishnu. Wherever Vishnu incarnates, Lakshmi follows, adapting herself to the circumstances of the age. This reflects a deeper truth in Hindu thought: divine energy does not simply exist in isolation but moves in harmony with the forces of creation and preservation. The feminine principle, embodied in Lakshmi, must always balance and complement the masculine, ensuring the flow of abundance, fertility, and divine grace.

This is an aspect I used in my Furies books, she incarnated to meet with Vishnu, but he was delayed in finding her, so she was married off to another. Whoops. A child was born, who was now a demi-god. Which helped the plot along nicely.

One of her most well-known avatars is Sita, the queen of Ayodhya and the devoted wife of Rama. In the Ramayana, Sita's story is one of unwavering devotion, sacrifice, and resilience. She is not simply Lakshmi in another body—she is Lakshmi adapted to the conditions of a world where dharma, duty, and suffering shape the course of events. Sita's trials, from exile in the forest to her abduction by Ravana, represent the struggles of divine energy when immersed in the human world. She is prosperity placed under hardship; fortune tested by fate. When she ultimately returns to the earth, it signifies that divine abundance is not something to be possessed but something that must be honored and respected. When neglected or mistreated, it withdraws.

Lakshmi also takes form as Rukmini, the chief consort of Krishna. Where Sita represents endurance and sacrifice, Rukmini embodies the joyous and sovereign aspects of

Lakshmi's nature. Unlike Sita, who suffers under the weight of dharma, Rukmini seizes her own destiny. She chooses Krishna, defying convention by writing to him and arranging her own rescue from an unwanted marriage. This aspect of Lakshmi reveals a different facet of divine fortune—one that is not merely bestowed upon the worthy but actively pursued by those who recognize its value. Rukmini's role in Krishna's life is not one of quiet suffering but of active participation in divine play (lila). She is not a test of faith but a reward for understanding the true nature of divine love.

The forms of Lakshmi are not limited to benevolence. As much as she represents abundance and prosperity, she also has a shadow side—one that appears as Alakshmi. While Lakshmi brings fortune, Alakshmi is the force of misfortune, poverty, and discord. They are not separate beings in opposition to each other; they are two sides of the same principle. Where Lakshmi arrives, bringing wealth and happiness, Alakshmi follows when greed, excess, or neglect of spiritual duty corrupts that wealth. This is why she is often associated with quarrels, bad luck, and strife within a household. The presence of Lakshmi is not simply about material riches but about harmony, generosity, and righteous action. Where these are absent, Alakshmi naturally takes over. In this way, Hindu thought acknowledges that fortune is not just about acquiring wealth—it is about maintaining balance. If prosperity is hoarded or abused, it ceases to be Lakshmi and becomes Alakshmi.

Beyond these well-known incarnations, Lakshmi takes on other forms, adapting to different needs and cosmic cycles. In some traditions, she is Bhudevi, the Earth itself, nourishing and sustaining life. Here, she is not just a goddess to be worshipped but the very foundation upon which all abundance depends. As Bhudevi, she teaches that prosperity is not something external to be accumulated but something deeply connected to the land, the seasons, and the cycles of nature. This is a form of Lakshmi that demands care and responsibility, reminding humanity that wealth is not separate from the environment that sustains it.

Another significant form is Shri, the abstract and primordial manifestation of Lakshmi's energy. Shri is not a personified goddess but the very essence of auspiciousness. The Vedic hymns speak of Shri as the divine radiance that brings success, fertility, and beauty. Unlike the later Puranic depictions of Lakshmi, where she is a distinct figure, Shri is more like a cosmic principle—a force that moves through those who align themselves with dharma and right action. This aspect of Lakshmi reveals the impersonal side of divine fortune: it does not play favorites, nor does it simply reward devotion. It follows those who act in harmony with universal law.

What unites all these forms is the idea that Lakshmi is not a static being but a fluid and responsive force. She manifests differently depending on the needs of the age, the people who call upon her, and the balance that must be restored. Unlike

Western depictions of gods who have fixed personalities and domains, Hindu deities shift and evolve. Lakshmi is not just a goddess of wealth—she is the force behind wealth, the intelligence that governs its flow, and the wisdom that determines its rightful use.

This fluidity is what allows Hinduism to integrate new manifestations of Lakshmi as cultural and spiritual needs change. In some regions, she is worshipped in unique local forms, each emphasizing different aspects of abundance. Some traditions merge her with other goddesses, recognizing that divine energy cannot be neatly categorized. The tantric traditions take this even further, seeing Lakshmi as a force that can be actively invoked and directed, not just through prayer but through specific rituals and meditative practices designed to attune the practitioner to her energy.

Lakshmi's many manifestations are a testament to the complexity of Hindu thought. They show that divinity is not rigid or singular but infinitely adaptable. Whether appearing as Sita, Rukmini, Bhudevi, or even as the shadowy Alakshmi, she is always responding to the needs of the world. To understand Lakshmi is to understand that fortune itself is not static—it is something that flows, shifts, and changes depending on how it is treated. Those who seek her blessings must recognize that wealth is not just material—it is spiritual, ethical, and deeply connected to the balance of life.

Karma & Reincarnation

My own take on Karma is that it is not punishment or reward—it's balance. It's the force that ensures energy moves where it is needed, aligning cause with effect, not as retribution but as a way to keep the universe in equilibrium. Every action, thought, and intention generates an imprint that eventually returns. But karma is not an inescapable fate. It is a system of balance, and balance can be shifted. This is where Lakshmi comes in.

Lakshmi is not just the goddess of wealth—she governs the flow of energy in all forms. Fortune is not random; it follows patterns. Some are inherited, some are self-created, but all can be altered. Where karmic cycles lock someone into scarcity, stagnation, or missed opportunities, Lakshmi's energy provides movement. She does not erase consequences, but she transforms how energy manifests, opening pathways where before there were only walls.

Karmic cycles tied to abundance are often unconscious. People repeat the same financial struggles, attract the same limitations, or experience success that vanishes just as quickly as it arrives. This is not some divine test or punishment—it is simply misalignment. The same force that creates stagnation can be redirected to create prosperity. Lakshmi, when properly invoked, reveals these patterns and offers a way to shift them.

Her presence highlights where energy is blocked. If wealth seems fleeting, if opportunities continually slip away, if there is a pattern of gaining only to lose—there is a karmic imbalance at play. Lakshmi does not simply bestow fortune; she aligns one's vibration with it. Working with her is not about demanding riches but about clearing the pathways that allow fortune to flow naturally. This is why true wealth is more than money—it is stability, opportunity, and the right circumstances appearing at the right time.

Lakshmi's ability to enhance or break karmic patterns is why offerings to her are not about bribery. They are about demonstrating an openness to change, an intention to realign. Acts of generosity, conscious financial decisions, and a willingness to shift old habits all serve as signals that the practitioner is ready to move out of stagnation. She does not reward greed, nor does she respond to desperation. Her energy flows to those who actively cultivate balance, those who recognize that wealth is not something external to be grasped but an energy to be harmonized with.

The key to working with Lakshmi is understanding that fortune is fluid. What appears as bad luck is often misdirected energy. What seems like an inescapable cycle is simply an unbroken pattern. Lakshmi does not force change—she presents the opportunities. Those who align with her energy find that fortune becomes a state of being rather than something to chase. Karma moves, balances, and shifts. With the right alignment, so does prosperity.

Lakshmi in Various Hindu Traditions

Lakshmi is one of the most widely revered deities in Hinduism, but her role shifts depending on the tradition through which she is viewed. She is never just a goddess of wealth—her presence extends into cosmic order, material and spiritual abundance, and the underlying force that sustains creation itself. How she is perceived depends on the theological framework through which she is approached. Among Shaivites, Vaishnavites, and Shaktas, Lakshmi takes on different aspects, not because she is separate in nature, but because the traditions emphasize different elements of the divine.

For Vaishnavites, Lakshmi is inseparable from Vishnu. She is his consort, his energy, his shakti—the force that empowers his cosmic role as the sustainer of the universe. In this view, Lakshmi is not an independent deity, nor does she function outside of Vishnu's influence. Instead, she is the embodiment of grace, the divine provider who ensures the world remains in harmony. Just as Vishnu descends in avatars to restore dharma, Lakshmi follows, incarnating as Sita, Rukmini, and other forms, always reflecting the needs of the age. She is the source of material prosperity but also the bestower of moksha, liberation, for those who recognize that true wealth is not found in possessions but in alignment with divine order.

Vaishnavite traditions place great emphasis on Lakshmi's role as the merciful mother, the intercessor who softens

Vishnu's judgments. She is the one who grants boons, answering prayers for both worldly success and spiritual upliftment. Temples dedicated to Vishnu always include her presence, because Vishnu without Lakshmi is incomplete. She is the divine balance, the nurturing aspect that ensures Vishnu's sustaining power flows to the world in an accessible form. Her energy is both practical and transcendent—she is the giver of fortune, but she is also Bhudevi, the very earth itself, making her the foundation upon which all prosperity rests.

Shaivites, however, do not place Lakshmi in such a central role. In Shaiva traditions, Shiva does not require a consort in the same way Vishnu does. While he has Parvati, Durga, and Kali as his shakti, they are not merely companions but embodiments of his power, existing both as separate and as aspects of himself. Lakshmi does not have the same prominence in Shaivism because Shiva's role is destruction and transformation—he is not a preserver of wealth or worldly order in the same way Vishnu is. However, this does not mean that Lakshmi is absent.

In some Shaivite traditions, Lakshmi is honored, but she is viewed as a secondary goddess, often as an extension of Parvati's nurturing aspect. Wealth, in the Shaiva worldview, is impermanent. Shiva, as the ascetic, does not seek prosperity, nor does he uphold the material world in the same way Vishnu does. For those who follow the Shaiva path, Lakshmi represents worldly attachments, something to be respected but ultimately transcended. Her gifts are necessary for life, but they are not the ultimate goal. The deeper purpose is liberation, and while Lakshmi can provide the means for a comfortable existence, true followers of Shiva see her blessings as tools rather than ends in themselves.

Despite this, Lakshmi appears even in Shaivite narratives. In tantric Shaivism, where energies are manipulated for both spiritual and material gain, Lakshmi becomes more relevant. Some traditions see her as a manifestation of kundalini, the latent energy that rises through the chakras, unlocking higher states of awareness. Here, her role is not just wealth but inner illumination—prosperity is not measured in gold but in spiritual attainment. This is where Lakshmi, even within a Shaivite framework, takes on a deeper esoteric meaning.

For Shaktas, Lakshmi is not just Vishnu's consort, nor is she secondary to Shiva's path of asceticism. She is an aspect of the great divine feminine, the supreme Shakti that moves through all things. Unlike Vaishnavites, who see her as Vishnu's balancing force, or Shaivites, who view her as a lesser presence, Shaktas recognize her as an independent power. She is not merely wealth—she is the creative force of the universe. She is abundance in its rawest form, the energy that sustains existence itself.

In Shakta traditions, Lakshmi is one of many faces of the Devi, the great goddess. She is one of the Mahavidyas, powerful expressions of divine feminine wisdom, and her role extends beyond mere fortune into deep spiritual transformation. Here, she is not a passive bestower of wealth but an active force that shapes reality. She is invoked not just for material gain but for the ability to control and direct the flow of prosperity. This is why Lakshmi has a strong presence in tantric practices—her energy is one of attraction, magnetism, and the mastery of abundance.

Shakta perspectives also emphasize the balance between Lakshmi and her counterpart, Alakshmi. Just as the goddess Durga wields destruction alongside creation, Lakshmi carries both prosperity and misfortune within her. To invoke her without understanding her dual nature is to misunderstand her entirely. In this tradition, working with Lakshmi is not about asking for riches—it is about tuning into the energetic reality of abundance itself. She becomes a force of manifestation, a conscious and directed power rather than a deity passively granting wishes.

Across these traditions, Lakshmi shifts but never loses her essence. To Vaishnavites, she is the nurturing mother, the soft power behind Vishnu's divine order. To Shaivites, she is a transient energy, useful but ultimately secondary to the pursuit of enlightenment. To Shaktas, she is a supreme force, an aspect of the great goddess herself, wielded with intention rather than simply worshipped. Each perspective reveals something different about her nature, showing that divine energy is not static but fluid, adapting to the consciousness of those who seek it.

Ultimately, Lakshmi is not bound by any one tradition.

She moves between them, taking on the form that best serves those who call upon her. Whether seen as Vishnu's consort, a force to be transcended, or the very embodiment of abundance itself, she remains the same energy—shaping, guiding, and flowing wherever she is honored.

CHAPTER 2

Lakshmi in Hindu Religions: Origins & Myths

Okay, here's some additional information on this fascinating goddess. Since she's featured in countless texts and popular stories, let's explore her origins and myths.

Lakshmi's presence in Hindu tradition stretches far beyond the well-known myth of the churning of the ocean. While that tale solidified her as the goddess of wealth and fortune, many lesser-known stories shape the way she is understood and worshipped across different regions. These myths reveal not just her generosity but also the conditions she sets for her presence. Lakshmi does not indiscriminately bestow wealth—she is selective, drawn to certain energies and repelled by others. Her nature is fluid, moving between households, villages, and individuals based on alignment with her essence.

One of the most telling myths comes from South Indian traditions, where Lakshmi is seen as a wandering goddess. Unlike Vishnu, who is stable, constant, and ever-present, Lakshmi moves. She chooses where to stay based on the purity of the space and the intent of those who seek her blessings. In certain folk stories, she enters a household only if it is clean, peaceful, and filled with reverence. A disordered home, filled with arguments and negativity, drives her away. This belief extends into household customs—sweeping the house at dusk is often avoided, as it is believed that one might inadvertently drive Lakshmi out. A well-lit entrance is seen as an invitation for her to enter. These practices are not just superstition; they come from the deeper understanding that wealth, in its truest form, thrives in order, harmony, and intention.

In some variations of this myth, Lakshmi is said to be a restless deity who dislikes staying in one place for too long. When a person or family becomes too attached to their wealth, hoarding it without generosity or gratitude, she slips away. This belief is particularly strong in Maharashtra, where Lakshmi Puja is not just about calling her in, but about maintaining her favor. The rituals involve not just inviting her into the home, but keeping her comfortable so she stays. The idea that wealth is a flow, rather than something to be trapped and locked away, comes directly from these stories. Hoarded wealth is dead wealth, and Lakshmi moves where energy circulates freely.

Lakshmi's association with marriage carries similar themes of balance, movement, and intention. In many regions, she is invoked during wedding ceremonies to ensure not just material prosperity but harmony between the couple. Marriage is considered one of the most significant ways Lakshmi enters a household, and the treatment of the bride mirrors the way Lakshmi herself is revered. In traditional Tamil Nadu weddings, the bride is seen as a manifestation of Lakshmi, and her first steps into her husband's home are ritualized to ensure the prosperity she brings remains. If she is welcomed with love, respect, and care, Lakshmi is believed to stay in the household, blessing it for generations. If she is mistreated, wealth and harmony dissolve.

In another regional tale from Odisha, Lakshmi leaves the home of Lord Jagannath, furious at his neglect. The story describes how, once she departs, the divine household falls into disorder. Food becomes scarce, and even the gods suffer from the loss of her presence. Only after sincere repentance does she return, restoring abundance. This myth reinforces a crucial aspect of her nature—her favor is conditional. She is a goddess who must be respected, not merely worshipped. Wealth, in all its forms, is not guaranteed. It is the result of alignment with the principles she embodies: generosity, integrity, and reverence.

Perhaps the most striking variations of Lakshmi's myths

come from Bengal, where she is sometimes depicted in a more independent light. In certain folk traditions, she is not simply the consort of Vishnu but a self-sufficient force, choosing where to go based on merit rather than devotion alone. In some versions of Lakshmi's stories, she is said to test people before bestowing her blessings. A man may pray for wealth, but if his actions show greed, dishonesty, or arrogance, Lakshmi withholds her gifts. In these tales, she is not just a passive bringer of fortune but an active force of judgment, deciding who is worthy.

One particular story speaks of a poor but kind-hearted woman who offers food to a wandering sage. Unbeknownst to her, the sage is an incarnation of Lakshmi herself, testing human nature. Seeing the woman's selflessness despite her own hardships, Lakshmi blesses her with unending abundance. This theme is echoed in many regions— Lakshmi's favor is not won through empty rituals but through genuine virtue. Wealth follows those who embody the principles she values: generosity, gratitude, and ethical conduct.

Lakshmi's nature is also closely tied to the cycles of the land, and in agricultural societies, she is deeply linked to the harvest. In many rural traditions, she is worshipped not in temples but in the fields. Farmers believe that Lakshmi walks the land during the growing season, ensuring prosperity. If the land is well cared for, she stays. If greed leads to overexploitation, she departs, leaving the fields barren. This understanding of her as a force of balance extends beyond just money—she is the sustainer of all forms of abundance, requiring care and reciprocity.

Another little-known but significant belief tied to Lakshmi is her connection to time. She is sometimes associated with fleeting opportunities, where fortune must be recognized and acted upon quickly. In certain Marathi traditions, it is said that Lakshmi knocks on one's door only once. If ignored, she moves on. This is not just about physical wealth but about recognizing and seizing the right moments in life. Hesitation, laziness, or complacency cause her to slip away. This aspect of her nature reinforces the idea that fortune favors the bold, the prepared, and the aware.

In direct opposition to the benevolent Lakshmi, stands Alakshmi, a representation of the negative aspects of existence, namely misfortune, destitution, and avarice. If Lakshmi is the radiant flow of prosperity, abundance, and auspiciousness, Alakshmi is the stagnant, grasping void that swallows wealth, leaving behind scarcity and discord. She is not an enemy of Lakshmi, nor a mere absence of fortune—she is a presence in her own right, moving alongside her sister, ensuring that where one thrives, the other lingers just beyond reach. Their interplay defines the cycle of gain and loss, generosity and avarice, wealth and ruin.

Alakshmi's origins mirror those of Lakshmi. Both arose from the churning of the cosmic ocean, the great act of divine upheaval that brought forth both treasures and poisons. But while Lakshmi emerged as beauty and grace, embodying the fortune of creation, Alakshmi came forth carrying the weight of its darker counterpart. She is associated with strife, deprivation, and all that twists prosperity into ruin. In the myth, Lakshmi chooses to align with the gods, bringing her gifts to those who uphold order and dharma, while Alakshmi moves toward the asuras, the beings who often embody unchecked desire and rebellion against divine balance. Yet her presence is not limited to demons or the wicked—she exists wherever greed overtakes generosity, wherever resentment festers, wherever imbalance invites the slow corrosion of wealth.

She is depicted as thin, aged, her body a sharp contrast to the lush curves of Lakshmi. Where Lakshmi's presence is adorned in gold and bright silks, Alakshmi's form is often described as dark and haggard, clothed in rags, sometimes riding a donkey, the beast of burden that trudges through barren lands. Some depictions give her wild, unkempt hair, a perpetual scowl, her mouth twisted in bitterness. She does not radiate light—she drains it, leaving behind an atmosphere of decay. Where she walks, discord follows. Her arrival is not always immediate catastrophe; often, she erodes rather than destroys, her influence creeping into households, into relationships, into minds. She turns abundance into hoarding, security into paranoia, contentment into endless dissatisfaction. She does not simply take wealth—she warps it, ensuring that even in its presence, there is no joy.

This is why Alakshmi is associated not just with poverty, but with greed itself. The miser who clutches gold yet lives in fear of losing it is as much under her shadow as the one who has nothing at all. Lakshmi's wealth flows, moving in and out of hands, circulating, feeding prosperity. Alakshmi's wealth stagnates, piling up in vaults where it does no good, or slipping through fingers no matter how tightly one tries to hold on. She is the force that whispers that nothing is ever enough, that more is always needed, that security is an illusion unless one hoards everything for oneself. She thrives in excess as much as in deprivation. The one who fears losing wealth, the one who cannot stop chasing more, the one who resents the fortune of others—these are all caught in Alakshmi's grasp.

Her presence is not always a curse, but a consequence. She comes where she is invited, where the conditions allow her to settle in. Households filled with quarrels, resentment, and stinginess will find her taking up residence. Her name is invoked when fortune turns sour, when businesses fail, when homes fall into disrepair, when food spoils before it can be eaten. She is misfortune in all its forms, but more than that, she is the root cause of it. The undoing of prosperity is not always random. It begins with the mind, with the heart, with the choices made in the pursuit of wealth.

Yet she is not omnipresent. Where generosity thrives, where people act with gratitude and openness, her grip weakens. Lakshmi and Alakshmi do not inhabit the same space at the same time. One is drawn where the other is repelled. In many traditions, Alakshmi is driven away through acts of purification—homes are cleansed, offerings are made, bitterness is cast out. This is not superstition; it is a deep understanding of how fortune and misfortune work. Wealth is not just about accumulation but about movement, about flow. When one clings too tightly, when selfishness overtakes generosity, when fear rules one's relationship with abundance, misfortune takes root.

She is invoked, not to be worshipped, but to be warded off. In many households, rituals are performed to banish her presence before welcoming Lakshmi in. Her symbols—bitter foods, harsh sounds, cracked vessels—are used to represent all that must be cast out before fortune can take its place. This is most evident in the traditions surrounding Lakshmi's festivals, where the two sisters are acknowledged together, one repelled so that the other may be received.

Lakshmi's Festivals

I love a good festival. The press of the crowds, the music, the colors. I can be found at most local festivals, but I haven't attended festivals in India. So, the following info is gleaned from multiple sources online.

Lakshmi's presence in Hindu festivals isn't just about celebration—it's about access. These aren't just holidays where people throw flowers at statues and light a few lamps.

These festivals are like open doors, moments when her energy is at its strongest, easiest to connect with, and most willing to settle into the lives of those who know how to welcome her in. Among all the ways she's honored, two stand out: Diwali, the festival of lights, and Varalakshmi Vratam, a day of deep devotion to securing her blessings. These aren't just religious events; they're powerful rituals that align people with the current of fortune and abundance.

Diwali is probably the best-known, but a lot of people don't realize what's actually happening on that night. It's not just about fireworks or pretty decorations—it's about clearing space for Lakshmi to arrive. It's the moment every year when the energy of prosperity is at its highest, when everything aligns just right for fortune to flow in. The myths surrounding it all point to the same thing: the triumph of light over darkness, of renewal over destruction. One story says Lakshmi emerged from the ocean on this night, rising from the depths after a cosmic battle, bringing divine wealth with her. Another version ties it to Vishnu's victory over a demon king, where Lakshmi arrives after the chaos is wiped away. Either way, the message is clear—fortune only enters where there's space for it.

That's why Diwali starts with a deep cleanse. Homes are scrubbed, clutter is thrown out, floors are washed. This isn't just about having a nice-looking house; it's a full energetic reset. Lakshmi doesn't stick around where things are messy, stagnant, or neglected. Then come the lights—diyas, candles, everything glowing. Darkness is pushed back. Light isn't just symbolic here; it literally attracts her. Then the offerings—flowers, sweets, coins, and the all-important diya placed in front of her image. But this isn't about bribing a goddess with pretty things. It's an exchange, an alignment. People sit before her, prayers are spoken, mantras fill the space, and the energy shifts. This is the moment when she arrives, when her presence becomes real. Those who do this with full focus, full belief, full willingness to receive—they feel it. The air gets heavier, warmer, alive.

But here's the thing—Diwali isn't just about asking for wealth. It's about understanding it. Lakshmi's gifts don't just go to whoever begs the loudest. She's drawn to generosity, to gratitude, to those who know how to use fortune wisely. The richest people in the world can still be drowning in misfortune if they don't understand this. Hoarding, greed, fear of losing—it's all tied to Alakshmi, the other side of this coin. Lakshmi flows where there's movement. Give and receive. Respect what you have. Keep things in balance. That's the true magik of Diwali.

Then there's Varalakshmi Vratam, which works a little differently. If Diwali is about opening the floodgates, this one is about securing Lakshmi's presence, making sure her blessings aren't fleeting but stay anchored in life. This festival, mostly celebrated in South India, is all about honoring her many forms—wealth, knowledge, courage, power, success, family, and nourishment. Because real fortune isn't just about money. What's the point of wealth if you don't have health? Or love? Or the strength to hold onto what you've built?

On this day, women fast, pray, and perform rituals to bring Lakshmi's energy directly into their homes. The centerpiece of it all is the kalasha—a sacred pot filled with water, decorated with gold, flowers, and topped with a coconut to represent Lakshmi herself. This isn't just a symbol; it's a vessel for her energy. It holds the essence of abundance in all forms. The whole point of this festival is to make sure that once Lakshmi is invited in, she stays. It's a way to lock in prosperity, to create a steady, lasting flow instead of just a momentary blessing.

The thing with these festivals is that they don't just end when the lights are turned off or the offerings are taken away. They aren't just about that one day—they set the tone for everything that follows. People who truly understand Lakshmi's energy don't just worship her once a year; they live in a way that keeps her presence strong. They keep their spaces clear, their energy open, their wealth moving instead of stagnating. They give before they take. They respect what they have. They trust in the flow of fortune, rather than trying to strangle it with fear.

These aren't just holidays. They're activations. Powerful moments when Lakshmi's energy is easiest to reach, when her lessons are clearest, when her presence is strongest. For those who know how to work with them, they're more than tradition—they're transformation.

Lakshmi and the Star-Born Archive

I didn't read this in a book.

I recovered it. From the quiet between mantras. From the stillness after flame. From the voice that speaks only after you've given up needing answers.

That's when she came. Lakshmi.

She didn't appear as a distant deity. She arrived like memory. Like something I already knew and had only forgotten. A golden resonance, older than language, flowing through the bones of the Earth and the spiral inside every galaxy.

Lakshmi is far more than a goddess of wealth. That's just the front-facing role. The mask she wears for those who still see the world through the lens of coin and grain. But her true current—what moves behind the symbol—is a harmonic stabilizer from before the flood. A cosmic archivist from a time when memory was stored in mantra, fire, and sound.

The Hindu mythos is more than it seems. It's a survivor record. A disguised technology. A galactic memory net that was spread across this planet after a cataclysm—meant to keep the codes alive until we were ready to remember. Lakshmi is one of the keepers of that memory.

She came through the Deva Confederation. Not metaphorically—literally. These were Andromedan-aligned beings, working with the Lyran and Pleiadian councils to preserve knowledge after the collapse of Dwaraka, Mu, and other ancient centers. Lakshmi arrived with encoded frequencies. Her energy wasn't wealth—it was rhythm. Order. Spiral harmony.

She didn't bring treasure. She brought resonance. Cycles. Balanced flow.

It's why her presence is felt strongest when everything is clean, symmetrical, and aligned. She is attracted not to need— but to coherence. Rituals done with cluttered minds and chaotic space rarely reach her. But when your energy field is smooth, when your inner rhythm matches the pulse of stars, she notices.

She sees through your walls. She feels the spiral inside your breath.

In trance, I saw the Shri Yantra not just as sacred geometry—but as a working machine. A harmonic resonance grid built from ancient star knowledge. Lakshmi flows through this spiral like water through a circuit. When you chant her names—Shri, Shreem, Maha Lakshmi—you're not just praying. You're running a command code.

Mantra is software. Sanskrit was never just a language. It's a vibrational matrix designed to link your consciousness to higher fields. To remember. To reawaken the dormant links to star ancestry.

Lakshmi's presence is encoded in those mantras. She is part of a system meant to stabilize your field and activate your capacity to receive—not just wealth, but cosmic order. When you align with her, your life organizes itself into abundance. Not because she grants it. Because she is it.

One night during ritual, I saw her fully. Not as a statue. Not as a robed goddess. But as light. Shifting geometries. A being seated within a rotating galactic spiral, holding waveforms in her hands. Behind her stood luminous presences—some humanlike, some not. Naga beings. Arcturian harmonics. They watched, silent, as she wove threads of energy from her palms into the fabric of space.

She looked at me—not with eyes, but with recognition.

And in that moment, I remembered my part.

I was there. During the early seeding. I helped anchor the fire ceremonies that would become the Vedas. I encoded spiral harmonics into the chants. We sang not to worship—but to preserve. We burned offerings not to please—but to broadcast. Lakshmi was always near those fires, guiding the energy, tuning the gates.

If you feel drawn to her now, it's not random.

She's calling back those who helped build the network. The ones who walked away when the frequencies collapsed, but who swore to return. And now is that time. The old codes are waking. The Earth's field is shifting. And Lakshmi is here to help stabilize the new wave.

But she won't respond to begging.

She responds to alignment.

Your breath. Your voice. Your will. In harmony.

Sing to her not for gold—but to remember. Offer not for

favor—but to activate. And let your ritual become a key—not a plea.

Because this isn't worship.

It's recovery.

Ritual: Reawakening Lakshmi's Harmonic Archive

This isn't a spell. It's a signal. You're tuning yourself like an instrument. When you're in harmony, she arrives.

This ritual works best after sunset on a Friday. But if the feeling comes strong, do it then. Don't wait.

Items Needed:

- Two white altar candles (for balance and purity)
- One gold or yellow ritual candle (for Lakshmi's waveform)
- Sandalwood incense (carrier of star memory)
- A printed or drawn Shri Yantra (place this at the center)
- Small bowl of rose petals or uncooked rice (offering of flow or sustenance)
- Your petition (optional: one line asking to remember and restore your alignment with her codes)

Ritual Steps:

Clean your space. Physically and energetically. You're

entering a signal chamber.

Light the incense. Let it rise like breath from the Earth.

Light the altar candles. One to your left. One to your right. Then light the gold ritual candle in front of the Shri Yantra.

Sit quietly. Breathe in through your nose, out through your mouth. Count twelve slow breaths. Let your mind empty.

Place your hands over the Shri Yantra. Whisper this chant:

"Shreem Shriyei Namaha"

Say it slowly. As many times as you feel. Let it settle into your chest like a tuning fork.

Close your eyes. Visualize Lakshmi not as a person—but as light spiraling from the center of the Yantra. Let her presence stabilize your mind and breath.

Speak aloud:

"Lakshmi, keeper of rhythm, stabilizer of worlds,
open the archive I once sang into the fire.
Let the golden current move through me again.
May I remember. May I realign."

Offer the petals or rice to the base of the Yantra. With your right hand. Slowly. One handful or one pinch at a time. Each motion seals the signal.

Sit in silence. Let any images, words, or feelings rise. You may receive something subtle. You may not. Doesn't matter. You've already transmitted.

Blow out the candles in reverse order. Gold candle first. Then the white ones.

After 24 hours, take the offering outside. Leave it beneath

a tree, in a garden, or near water. Return it with no attachment. You've done your part.

This ritual reawakens the harmonic link. If done once with clarity, it can activate memory for months. If done weekly, it becomes a golden spiral that reorganizes your life around abundance and flow.

CHAPTER 3

Lakshmi's Powers - Both Popular and lesser known

Wealth and prosperity.

Lakshmi is often called upon to bring prosperity, but her power is not as simple as bestowing wealth upon those who ask. It's not a transactional exchange. She doesn't just grant financial gains; she shifts the entire energetic field around an individual, aligning them with the frequency of abundance. Those who truly understand her power know that Lakshmi doesn't merely give—she teaches how to become wealth, how to anchor it into every layer of existence, so it is not fleeting but sustained.

Attracting wealth isn't about luck. It's about magnetism, about creating an energetic pull so strong that wealth, in all its forms, naturally gravitates toward the practitioner. Lakshmi's energy moves through patterns of flow and stability. Wealth isn't meant to come in short bursts and vanish; it's meant to be an ever-flowing river. Many misunderstand this and focus only on the receiving aspect, never considering that true wealth is something cultivated internally before it manifests externally. Lakshmi's presence shifts the mind into a state of constant openness to prosperity. This is what separates those who temporarily experience abundance from those who live in abundance.

This is where wealth consciousness becomes essential. Lakshmi's influence restructures the way one interacts with the concept of wealth itself. She dissolves poverty consciousness, the deeply ingrained fear that money is hard to obtain or will inevitably be lost. That fear is what keeps people trapped in cycles of scarcity. A mind programmed for lack will reject wealth even when it arrives, sabotaging opportunities, avoiding financial decisions, or unconsciously pushing money away. Lakshmi clears this energetic debris, replacing it with a state of reception. When one is truly aligned with her energy, money is no longer something that must be chased—it is something that flows toward them effortlessly.

Mantra work is one of the most effective ways to shift into this frequency. Lakshmi's bija mantra, Shreem, carries the vibrational essence of abundance. Chanting it consistently tunes the body and mind to the energy of wealth, making the practitioner a conduit for prosperity. But mantra alone is not enough. It must be paired with an understanding of how to hold that energy. Ritual baths infused with her essence—using saffron, lotus petals, and gold-infused water—physically imprint her presence onto the body, creating a direct connection between the practitioner and her realm. This ritual is not about purification in the conventional sense; it is about aligning the physical vessel with her frequency so that it can receive and retain prosperity.

Sacred geometry is another method to integrate Lakshmi's energy. The Sri Yantra, one of the most powerful symbols of wealth and manifestation, is deeply connected to her. It is a map of reality itself, a blueprint for creating and sustaining abundance. Meditating on the Sri Yantra, tracing its patterns with intention, or even keeping it in the home shifts the energetic field, making it more conducive to wealth. It is a direct link to Lakshmi's essence, a geometric form that encodes the principles of creation and expansion.

Beyond personal wealth, Lakshmi's power extends into the realm of objects, anchoring prosperity into the physical world. Certain items, when properly charged with her energy, become vessels of attraction. Gold coins, jewelry, banknotes—these can be transformed into talismans that pull wealth toward their owner. This is not superstition but a direct application of energetic principles. Just as a stone can hold heat, an object can hold the frequency of abundance when properly infused with it. In later chapters, we will explore the specific methods for this, ensuring that wealth, once attracted, remains.

Lakshmi's influence is cyclical, moving in rhythms that mirror the natural world. Her presence is strongest during certain times of the year, aligning with the cosmic tides of abundance. This is why her festivals are not merely cultural events; they are energetic openings where her power is most accessible. These celebrations, particularly Diwali, act as portals where practitioners can more easily connect with her, reinforcing the energetic shifts they have already cultivated. The timing of these rituals is not arbitrary—it is designed to synchronize with the natural flow of Lakshmi's energy, amplifying its effects in ways that are otherwise difficult to achieve.

Shifting Fate Through Karmic Realignment

Lakshmi's power extends far beyond wealth. She is a force that can shift fate itself, altering the trajectory of one's life by dissolving the weight of karmic debt. Many assume karma is an unchangeable force, something written in stone that dictates the highs and lows of a lifetime. But karma isn't fixed—it is an active, shifting energy, one that can be balanced, purified, and redirected. Lakshmi, as the embodiment of divine fortune, governs this process.

Her ability to realign fate comes through her connection to Vishnu, the preserver of cosmic order. Where Vishnu maintains dharma, Lakshmi brings the necessary adjustments that allow someone to step into prosperity without being chained to past misdeeds or unfortunate circumstances. Karma, in its essence, is a reflection of past choices, thoughts, and inherited patterns. It isn't just about past lives; it's about the accumulation of energy over time, shaping the reality one experiences. This is why some people seem destined for struggle while others naturally attract ease. Lakshmi's energy offers a way to reset this momentum.

She does not erase karma in the way one might wishfully hope—she won't simply cancel debts because someone lights a candle in her name. But she does open the path for karmic purification, allowing past burdens to be dissolved when the soul aligns with her frequency of abundance. Those who work with her seriously, with the intention of transformation, find that obstacles once deemed inevitable begin to shift. A person locked in financial struggle due to inherited beliefs about scarcity may suddenly find opportunities arising. Someone weighed down by repeated misfortunes—failed ventures, broken relationships, unforeseen losses—may notice a change in the rhythm of their life, as if something heavy has been lifted.

The key to this shift is punya, or spiritual merit. Lakshmi is deeply connected to this concept, as her gifts are not random; they are drawn to those who cultivate a mindset and energy field that mirrors her own. Punya is not just about good deeds—it is about purity of intent, clarity of purpose, and the willingness to release attachments to past wounds. This is why working with Lakshmi for karmic realignment is not about pleading for luck but about stepping into alignment with her essence. It requires a conscious release of outdated patterns, a willingness to let go of limiting beliefs, and an openness to receive her energy without resistance.

One of the most powerful ways to engage with Lakshmi's karmic realignment is through invoking her aspect of Vishnupriya. This form of Lakshmi is particularly tied to dharma and merit, making her an ideal force for dissolving past burdens and clearing the path forward. A ritual to invoke Vishnupriya Lakshmi focuses on purification, resetting life's trajectory toward abundance by unbinding the energetic knots of past missteps. It begins with preparing the space—white flowers, clarified butter, and rice symbolizing purity and sustenance. The practitioner lights a deepam, a traditional oil lamp, to represent the dissolution of ignorance and the illumination of new possibilities. The mantra 'Om Shri Vishnupriye Namaha' is chanted, each repetition peeling away the layers of stored karma, redirecting the course of fate.

The process of purification is not instant, nor is it passive. Working with Lakshmi in this way is an act of participation— she clears the path, but one must step forward. There may be moments of resistance, echoes of old patterns attempting to reassert themselves. But those who persist, who commit to embodying the energy of abundance rather than simply requesting it, find that their reality shifts. The unseen weight of karmic burdens begins to lift, and the flow of prosperity, once blocked by invisible forces, moves freely again.

Lakshmi's role in karma is one of empowerment. She does not grant wealth arbitrarily, nor does she pity those who claim to be cursed by fate. She offers a way out, a method of restructuring life's patterns so that fortune is not an occasional visitor but a constant presence. Understanding this aspect of her power transforms the way one works with her—it is no longer about fleeting requests for material gain but about engaging in a profound spiritual process. Real wealth, after all, is not just financial; it is the freedom to shape one's life without being bound by past limitations.

And this is where Lakshmi's presence is most felt—not just in the rituals, the mantras, or the carefully placed offerings, but in the lived experience of those who walk with her. The shift may start subtly: a sudden clarity about what must be released, an unexpected opportunity where none existed before, a feeling of ease replacing long-standing struggle. But over time, the transformation becomes undeniable. The trajectory of life moves toward prosperity, not as a random stroke of luck, but as an inevitable consequence of being in alignment with Lakshmi's energy.

This ability to shift fate, to dissolve the weight of past burdens, is one of Lakshmi's most profound gifts. But just as important as her ability to alter destiny is the way she is celebrated—the recognition of her presence through the great festivals that honor her. These celebrations are not just rituals of devotion; they are moments of energetic convergence, where entire communities align themselves with her abundance. The greatest of these is Diwali, the festival of lights, where Lakshmi is welcomed into homes to bring prosperity for the year ahead. But her presence extends beyond this well-known event, into lesser-known but equally potent celebrations that call upon her power in ways few understand.

Clearing the Way—How Lakshmi Removes Spiritual Blockages and Brings Clarity

Most people think of Lakshmi and immediately jump to wealth. Coins. Gold. That lovely cascade of abundance she's always shown pouring from her palms. But the truth is, her power starts long before that. Lakshmi doesn't just hand you treasure. She clears the damn path so you can even see where it is.

Her energy works like light through murky water. Not aggressive. Not forceful. Just calm, steady illumination that reveals the truth.

That's where we start.

When you call Lakshmi, you're not just asking for external riches. You're asking her to illuminate the riches you've buried inside yourself. And here's the kicker—most of us are walking around clogged with spiritual debris. Old pain. Family patterns. Religious fear. Shame. False humility that someone jammed into our heads when we were too young to say, "No thanks."

She doesn't blow it all out like a wrecking ball. She doesn't work that way.

Her clarity moves like silk sliding across skin. You might not even realize she's doing it—until you suddenly see things differently. That fight you had last week? Not yours. That feeling of being stuck in a loop? It starts to unravel. Not because she yells, but because she shows. And what she shows is where the blockage lives.

Most of the time, it's lodged in the mind first. That's where she begins her sweep. You might feel this as a sudden quiet in your thoughts after invoking her. A blankness. Stillness. Don't mistake that for emptiness. That's the pause where her light filters in.

I've seen her work on people who thought they were beyond help. People addicted to struggle. Addicted to poverty, even. She came in through a candle flame, or a simple chant, or a quiet offering of jasmine and sandalwood. And then? Boom. Not a lightning bolt—just a change of view. A mental reframe so clean it felt like the window had been washed for the first time in years.

Clarity is her true wealth.

When you have clarity, you stop chasing ghosts. You stop playing small. You stop doing rituals for money when what you really need is to cut a toxic tie or forgive yourself for something that's been festering in your chest for a decade.

Now here's something lesser-known. Lakshmi isn't just about flow—she's also a guardian. If something is blocking you, she won't just remove it and let the wind rush in. She stands watch over that space until **you** are strong enough to walk through. She doesn't leave it exposed. That's one of her quietest powers. She waits for you to be ready.

And when you are? She shows you where to go next.

Not with a GPS voice in your head, but through signs. Through small nudges. Through what looks like coincidence—but isn't. A door opens. A new person appears. You overhear something in a store that sticks in your head for a week. Her clarity comes threaded into the fabric of your day, but it's unmistakable when you tune in.

You'll know it's her because it feels clean. Not like pressure. Not like force. Like knowing. Like, ***Oh. Right. That's the move.***

Let me give you one personal example.

I once lit a candle to Lakshmi not for wealth, but for truth. I was tangled in a mess. Couldn't tell what was mine and what was projection. I didn't even ask her a question. Just lit the flame and sat.

What came next wasn't a vision. It wasn't a cosmic voice. It was a soft, persistent awareness that I'd been lying to myself—pretending something was working when it wasn't. No blame. Just truth. And with that came the unblocked energy to move. I ended something I'd been dragging out for months. A day later, I had a new client. Three days later, an unexpected gift showed up in the mail.

Clarity creates movement. That's how she works.

If you're stuck, call her. But don't start by begging for money. Ask her to clear the junk first. Ask her to show you what's in the way.

Sit in front of a white candle. Offer a single flower. Say:

"Goddess Lakshmi, remover of shadows, light my path. Show me what blocks my flow. Let me see with your eyes."

And then? Be quiet. Let her in. You might cry. You might laugh. You might just feel still. But after that? Things shift. It's not showy, but it's real. And once you see clearly— wealth becomes easy. Not just the money kind. The life kind. The truth kind.

And that's what she really brings.

Hidden Roles Lakshmi Plays in Hinduism

Her Role in Diplomacy, Sovereignty, and Cosmic Balance

Lakshmi isn't just the goddess of wealth. That's like saying the ocean is just wet. It's true—but it misses the whole damn picture.

Behind the gold coins and lotus petals, Lakshmi plays one of the most critical roles in Hindu cosmology. She doesn't just bless the empire—she holds it together.

Let's talk sovereignty.

In the older texts, Lakshmi is inseparable from kingship. Wherever she goes, legitimate rule follows. That's not symbolic. It's energetic. Her presence is the signal that the throne is in balance with cosmic order. In Sanskrit, they call this *Rta*—the truth that holds the universe in harmony. When a ruler falls out of that alignment, Lakshmi withdraws. That's when things fall apart. Crops fail. Fortunes reverse. Empires crack.

She doesn't fight. She leaves.

That's the power of her role. She's not the hammer. She's the balance point.

Diplomacy? She's the invisible hand.

In ancient times, kings and rulers would invoke Lakshmi not before battle—but before negotiation. Her energy softens the edges of pride. She reveals a path that serves both sides, not just the victor. She's not there to win arguments. She's there to prevent war.

I've felt this in ritual.

Call on her during a standoff—whether it's political or personal—and what happens next is eerie. People soften. Communication opens. You'll hear someone say something like, "I hadn't thought of it that way." That's her. Moving between hearts like wind between temple columns.

She's not loud. But she's effective as hell. Now the deeper layer—cosmic balance. Lakshmi's real role? She's the calibrator of flow across dimensions.

When the gods lose their way, when dharma itself goes wobbly, it's Lakshmi who recalibrates the system. You see this in the myth of the churning of the ocean—Samudra Manthan. All the gods and demons were out of balance, literally pulling in opposite directions. She emerges from the chaos. Not as a result—but as the solution.

She steps out of that primordial ocean like an answer. And with her presence comes amrita—the nectar of immortality. The literal balancing agent of divine and demonic forces.

So yeah. Not just coins.

She restores balance when the whole damn system tilts.

In practical terms?

She's the force you call when your life feels like a chessboard, and you're tired of pawns pretending they're kings. When diplomacy fails. When your own personal sovereignty's been hijacked. You call Lakshmi to reclaim your center.

She aligns you with what's true—not what looks good. Not what pleases everyone. What restores harmony to your field. Even if that means walking away from a deal, or pulling your energy from a system that's been draining you.

She doesn't yell. She withdraws. And when she withdraws from something? That thing falls apart.

If you're working with Lakshmi and feel her go quiet, check what you're aligning with.

She doesn't support domination. She supports harmony. If your path slips out of sync with your soul's truth—she'll wait. She's patient like the stars. But when you snap back into alignment? She returns full force. Flow resumes.

Ritual tip?

If you're facing power struggles—family, court, business—set up a candle in her name. White or gold. Offer something simple but pure. Honey. Milk. A lotus image. Sit and say:

"Lakshmi, keeper of true order—stand with me.

Guide me to wise action, noble truth, and rightful balance."

And then stop pushing. Let her adjust the field.

She won't scream. She won't argue. But you'll start seeing truths come to light. Lies slip. Hidden allies surface. Sometimes even enemies walk away confused, like they forgot why they were fighting.

That's her.

Sovereignty isn't about being the loudest. It's about being aligned. And Lakshmi? She's the source of that alignment when it matters most.

CHAPTER 4

Rituals to Lakshmi (Traditional Method)

If you go looking for Lakshmi rituals online or in temples, you'll find a lot of tradition. Centuries of repetition. The same mantras, the same images, the same setup. It works—but most of it wasn't made for people like us. Western magicians. Modern seekers. People without a Hindu priest on speed dial.

That doesn't mean it's wrong. It just means it's coded for a different time, place, and mindset.

Traditional Lakshmi rituals are beautiful. Structured. Overflowing with flowers, chants, color, offerings. The rituals are devotional, not demanding. You aren't summoning her—you're honoring her. You're creating a space so magnetic, so aligned, that she just steps in. Like a goddess walking through an open door into her own house.

Let's look at how that usually plays out.

The Setup: Beauty, Cleanliness, Intent

Lakshmi doesn't arrive where there's chaos, filth, or noise. In the traditional method, you clean the space first. Not just sweep the floor—you cleanse energetically. You bathe. You wear clean clothes. In many households, people fast, or avoid anger and conflict leading up to the ritual.

Your space becomes a small temple.

Then, you create an altar—sometimes simple, sometimes elaborate. A photo or statue of Lakshmi is placed in the center. Around it: flowers, fruit, gold coins, rice, turmeric, milk sweets, incense, candles or oil lamps.

If you're doing the full puja, you might have all sixteen classical steps. Most people today simplify. But the essence remains: beauty. Harmony. Respect.

Mantra: The Heartbeat of the Ritual

You don't talk to Lakshmi the way Western magicians might call on a spirit. You chant.

In traditional methods, mantras are everything. They're not just words. They're sound forms—encoded power. You repeat them 108 times, often with a mala bead strand. The repetition is a tuning fork. It shifts your energy, raises the vibration, and invites her to descend.

The most common one?

"Om Shreem Maha Lakshmiyei Namaha."

There are dozens more. Some long, some complex. But this one? It's the go-to. It covers prosperity, protection, and presence. The "Shreem" is a bija seed sound—pure Lakshmi energy, compressed into a single syllable.

You don't need to be fluent in Sanskrit. You need rhythm, focus, and sincerity.

Symbols and Yantras

Traditional Lakshmi rituals often use the Shri Yantra, either drawn by hand or placed on the altar. It's more than a symbol—it's a multidimensional map. The nine interlocking triangles form a sacred geometry pattern that represents both the cosmos and the goddess herself.

When you meditate on it, or chant to it, you're aligning with the pattern of creation.

Other yantras exist—some more focused on specific forms like Dhana Lakshmi (wealth), Gaja Lakshmi (abundance), or Vijaya Lakshmi (victory). Most are placed under or behind the image of the goddess. Some are charged with offerings, mantras, or even bathed in milk or rosewater.

They're not decorations. They're portals. Activators.

You don't need to understand all the details to feel their pull.

Just having one near during ritual changes the current.

Candles, Oil Lamps, and Incense

Traditionally, oil lamps are preferred. Ghee lamps, especially. But I've found that ritual candles work fine if the intention is clear. I use gold, green, or white. Lakshmi loves soft, glowing light. The kind that feels like home. If the room flickers with warmth and smells like a forest temple, you're on the right track.

And now—incense.

Let me tell you—this is my personal obsession. I've chased that perfect scent for years. The one that makes you feel like you've stepped into a 1970s metaphysical shop in Austin. Back when the shelves were cluttered, the incense was thick in the air, and someone was probably sitting cross-legged on a floor cushion reading Be Here Now.

Nag Champa was the scent of the era. But not all Nag Champa is equal. Most of what's out there now is flat. Too sweet, too chalky. The gold standard?

Everest Trader's Vintage Nag Champa.

That's the one. The real stuff. Deep, earthy, mellow. It lingers like a blessing.

I light it before anything else. That first swirl of smoke? That's your opening line. That's your signal to her: I'm here. I'm ready.

Offerings: Lakshmi's Language

In traditional settings, offerings matter. A lot. You're not bribing her—you're feeding the energy. You're matching her frequency.

Think sweet. Think golden. Think lush.

Common offerings include:

- Milk sweets (like peda or laddu)
- Fresh flowers (especially marigold or lotus)
- Scented oils
- Coins (real ones—don't get cute with Monopoly money)
- Rice or turmeric
- Wine (modern addition, but I include it often)
- Fruit (mango, banana, pomegranate)

You place them on the altar with love. You speak to her if you like. You ask. You thank. You don't demand.

And when the ritual ends, you either consume the offerings (called prasad), or release them into nature. No trash bins.

Time and Planetary Influences

Timing is real. You can feel it when you hit the right moment.

Friday is her core day. Ruled by Venus, aligned with beauty, prosperity, and love.

Thursday is also strong—linked to Jupiter, expansion, blessings.

Monday works when you're seeking peace in the home or healing energy. Use this when emotional blocks are in the way of wealth.

Work with the Moon cycle. Lakshmi energy rises strongest during the waxing moon. That's when you're building. Calling in.

The full moon is ideal for gratitude rituals. Anchor in the wealth you've already received.

During the new moon, go easy. Unless you're clearing out old energy, it's not the best time to call in abundance. Her current runs quiet then.

If you're astrology-savvy, time your rituals when Venus is strong or when there are trines to your natal Jupiter or Moon. But if that's not your thing, don't stress. Friday night, clean house, sweet incense, soft light—she'll show up.

Where My Methods Begin

Everything I've just laid out? It works. It's powerful. It's sacred.

But here's the thing.

You don't live in a temple. You don't always have the time or patience to follow sixteen steps, boil milk, or chant for hours. That doesn't mean Lakshmi won't work with you. It just means you need a different doorway.

That's where I come in.

In the next chapter, I'm going to show you how I've adapted her magik. How I take the bones of this traditional method and make them sing in the modern world. How I call her using my rhythm—without losing the power.

You'll still use incense. You'll still make offerings. But you'll shape it your way. And she'll come just as strong.

She's not bound to temples. She walks where she's welcome.

This is the kind of ritual that would be done on a Friday evening, with intention and beauty, but without a mountain of prep. Something the old aunties would do faithfully every week, and it worked.

Traditional Ritual to Lakshmi: Attracting Steady Financial Flow

Best time: Friday evening, during waxing moon

Duration: About 20–30 minutes

Intention: To invite a steady, dependable flow of money into your life—income, not a windfall

Items Needed:

- A clean white cloth (for your altar or surface)

- A framed image or small statue of Lakshmi
- A gold or green candle (substitute white if needed)
- Everest Trader's Vintage Nag Champa incense (or the best you've got)
- A small bowl of uncooked rice
- One coin (real currency)
- Fresh flowers (marigold, rose, or lotus if available)
- A small sweet (like a milk-based dessert, or honey-covered fruit)
- Optional: A printed Shri Yantra, placed under the coin or candle

Ritual Steps:

1.Clean the Space

Tidy the area. Wipe down surfaces. Lightly sweep or mop if needed. This clears stagnant energy and tells Lakshmi you're serious.

2. Set the Altar

Lay the white cloth down. Place Lakshmi's image at the center. Put the rice bowl in front of her, coin atop the rice. Arrange flowers beside her. Set the candle to one side, incense to the other.

3. Light the Incense First

As the smoke rises, whisper:

"May this sacred scent open the way to Lakshmi's presence."

4. Light the Candle

As you do, say:

"With this light, I welcome the presence of Maha Lakshmi, bringer of fortune and peace."

5. Chant the Mantra

Repeat the following 108 times (or 27 if time is short), counting with your fingers or a mala if you have one:

"Om Shreem Maha Lakshmiyei Namaha."

Let the sound settle into your body. You don't have to say it loudly—just with focus. Let each repetition be a soft knock at her door.

6. Make the Offering

Present the sweet, and say:

"Beloved Lakshmi, please accept this humble offering. I invite your blessings into my life. Let my income flow steady and strong, like a river that never runs dry."

7. Silent Moment

Close your eyes. Picture Lakshmi standing in your space,

golden light flowing from her hands. See the coin on your altar multiply. See money arriving, calmly and consistently. Not chaos—just smooth flow.

8. Close the Ritual

Thank her. Say:

"Lakshmi, I give thanks for what has come, what is coming, and what will always remain. Prosperity. Peace. Presence."

Let the candle burn a bit longer, then snuff it (don't blow it out). Leave the incense to finish.

Aftercare

You can eat the sweet or share it. Keep the coin in your wallet or on your altar—just don't spend it. Replace the flowers and rice weekly if you repeat the ritual. Over time, you'll notice her rhythm syncing with your finances.

CHAPTER 5

Lakshmi in My Magik Methods

Let's set the record straight. I don't follow traditional puja rites. I don't need a priest. I don't memorize 108 names or chant them while ringing a bell for two hours. That's not disrespect. That's just not how I connect.

Lakshmi is ancient. She doesn't need a script to know your heart.

When I work with her, it's not worship. It's magik. My kind of magik. Direct. Streamlined. Alive.

I kept what works and discarded what doesn't.

She didn't complain.

My Approach vs. Traditional Hindu Practices

Traditional ritual has rules. A lot of them.

What to wear. What to burn. Which mantra to use for which aspect of Lakshmi. The exact timing. The moon phase.

Whether you've bathed properly. Whether your altar is pure.

If you're raised in that system, it's a living current. Passed down through families. It hums with ancestral resonance. Beautiful, in its own way.

But for most people outside that world, it becomes a maze of rules and restrictions. And often, fear. "If I don't do this right, she won't come." "If I pronounce this mantra wrong, will I insult her?"

That fear has no place in real magik.

You don't need to be born into a Brahmin family to call Lakshmi. You just need to speak to her with truth.

In my work, ritual is stripped to the bones. It's not lesser—it's cleaner. I light candles. I burn incense. I speak with clear intent. I honor her with gifts. And then I open the door.

She doesn't need ancient Sanskrit to hear you.

She listens through vibration. She sees your frequency before you say a word.

Invocations: Chant vs. Command

Let's talk invocation.

In puja, it's recitation. Repetition. Precision. You chant to shift the mind. You chant to open the subtle gates. The mantras are a kind of access code—but they're coded for that system. They are beautiful, yes. But they're locked to an old language.

In my work, invocation is calling with power. It's not about how many times you say a word—it's about how you say it.

I speak her name like it matters. I project it. I align my field first—quiet the noise, gather my will, and then I speak. Sometimes loud. Sometimes a whisper.

Not with chanting lips—but with lit intention.

I don't ask. I don't plead. I don't follow a temple structure. I open the space and speak to her as a sovereign calling another sovereign.

"Lakshmi, Lady of Abundance, I welcome you into this circle.

Bring your flow. Bring your grace. Fill this space with gold and clarity."

Then I wait. And she comes.

The Energy When She Arrives

Here's what nobody tells you when they stick to book-based invocations—when she really arrives, you don't need to wonder if it worked.

You'll feel her.

Not like thunder. Not like fire. Like velvet. Like a golden wave brushing through your chest.

There's a softness to her that most people miss. You expect a goddess of wealth to roar in like a waterfall. But she doesn't. She moves with elegance.

She's smooth. She glides in. Her presence is sublime—yes, that word fits here.

It's not overwhelming. It's enveloping.

The air in the room changes. The edge of thought disappears. There's this quiet warmth, like being wrapped in a silk shawl that hums.

And then—clarity.

She brings clarity the way dawn brings light. No announcement. No trumpet. Just a quiet dissolving of doubt.

I'll often get that first wave of pressure behind the eyes, like energy settling behind my forehead. A warmth in the chest. A brief feeling of being watched—but not in a spooky way. Like someone sees all of you and still smiles.

There's a mother quality there. But not in the Earth Mother way. This is elegance. Refinement. The Mother who never makes you feel small.

She doesn't dominate the space. She graces it.

That's how you know it's her.

Working With Her Power: Energy vs. Prayer

In traditional prayer, you make requests. You list your needs. You hope she hears.

In magik, I don't hope. I align.

I shift my energy to match hers. I visualize gold—not coins, but energy. Liquid wealth. Flow. I see it rushing through my body like a current. I don't just ask her to give—I ask her to amplify what's already being built in my field.

This is key: Lakshmi doesn't just hand out checks. She enhances resonance.

If your field is full of fear, she won't punish you. But you won't magnetize much, either.

She brings what matches your flow.

So before I ever light a candle, I do the inner work. I clear resentment. I drop old beliefs about "money is bad" or "I'm not worthy." Then I anchor the truth: I am a magnet for what I choose to receive.

And Lakshmi? She steps in and wraps it in gold.

Rituals Outside of Time

Here's the other thing I love about working with her this way—she's not locked into auspicious hours.

Traditional work ties her to Fridays, full moons, Diwali, or Venus days. That's fine if you're into astrology-based timing. But I've called her on a random Tuesday at 3 a.m. and she answered just as strong.

Why? Because my field was open. Because the channel was clear.

Time doesn't matter when you're out of time.

Combining Her with Other Magikal Systems

Some people treat pantheons like rival high school cliques. I get this in emails all the time. Can I work with "X" and "Y"? Are they okay with it? As if calling Lakshmi in the same ritual with Clauneck or Lucifer will cause a divine turf war.

That's not how I work. And it's not how she works, either.

Lakshmi isn't territorial. She knows exactly who she is.

I've brought her into chaos magik. I've merged her field with Venusian planetary workings. I've asked her to bless money-based workings where daemons were handling the mechanics. She glides in without friction. She stabilizes. She adds sweetness to fire.

When I combine her and Lucifer? She tempers his blazing clarity with grace.

With Inanna? They blend like old friends—both powerful, both sovereign.

With Dantalion? She clears the emotional fog while he adjusts the mind.

She's the current of grace moving through complexity. She doesn't judge the system. She reads your energy. If you come correct—clear, open, focused—she joins.

That's why she fits in High Magik. Because High Magik isn't about form. It's about force. It's about building structure around energy.

And she is structured energy. Wealth, beauty, clarity, motion—given form.

Why It Works

This magik isn't about looking right. It's not about getting every detail perfect or reciting the "correct" mantra. It works because you're real. When you show up with reverence—not fear—she shows up. When your field is steady, your mind clear, and you speak her name with power, she listens.

Lakshmi isn't bound by dogma. She's moved through centuries of worship, crossed empires, adapted through ages. She knows when someone's putting on a show—and when someone is calling from a soul-deep place. She doesn't need perfection. She needs presence.

She's the river that knows her own path. You don't command her. You don't beg. You stand as a sovereign being and call her as an equal. And when you do, when you speak truthfully, when your energy is clean—she flows to you.

I don't need to be pure. I need to be clear. I don't need white robes, Sanskrit verses, or ghee on an altar. I need to mean every damn word I say. And when I do—she's there.

Always.

Bonus Ritual: The Whisper of Gold

Use this when you're stuck. When the money's not moving. When the energy feels foggy, blocked, or dull. This isn't a request. It's a reset. You're not asking Lakshmi for more. You're inviting her to sweep the dust out and get the flow moving again.

Items Needed

- One gold or yellow candle (a white candle will do in a pinch)
- Your favorite incense (Nag Champa, if you're like me)
- A bowl of clean water
- A coin (real or symbolic)
- Optional: a few drops of patchouli oil if you want to ground the working

Steps

Set your space

Keep it simple. Light the candle. Burn the incense. Place the water and coin in front of the candle. Let the setup breathe. This isn't a shrine—it's a signal.

Speak her name softly

Just say it once, with meaning.

"Lakshmi."

Pause. Feel the air shift.

Then:

"Clear the path. Restore the current. Let gold return."

Gaze into the water

Imagine the blocks dissolving. Picture your energy field

like a river—and see Lakshmi brushing away stones, twigs, old stories. The water becomes the field. The field becomes gold.

Whisper your need

Quietly, so only you and Lakshmi hear it. Keep it simple.
"I want clarity." Or "I want flow."
"I want peace with money." Or "I want my power back."
Say it how you mean it.

Drop the coin in the water

A signal. A shift. You're anchoring the request.

Sit in silence for three minutes

No mantras. Just stillness. Let her arrive.

If the air feels warmer, softer, or even heavy—she's already moving.

Blow out the candle

Not with force—just a breath. A release. A "thank you" without words.

Leave the bowl overnight if you can. Pour the water outside the next morning, and toss the coin into a place of movement—a river, a fountain, even a busy street if that's what you've got.

It's done.

CHAPTER 6

Wealth, Money Magik & Good Fortune

When people think of Lakshmi, they picture wealth—gold coins pouring from her hands, lotus flowers beneath her feet, and a face that radiates serenity. But what most don't understand is this: Lakshmi doesn't simply "give" you money. She's not a bank or a genie. Her energy is much more alive than that. When you invite her into your life, you're invoking a current. And that current doesn't respond to fear, desperation, or control. It moves toward clarity, alignment, beauty, and a subtle form of grace that can't be faked.

Wealth is motion. It's not static like a vault or a number in your account. It's energy that wants to move, to shift, to change hands, to grow. And Lakshmi rides that current. If your energy field is too blocked, cluttered, or filled with anxiety, the current slows down or bypasses you completely. You'll see others winning—succeeding, getting gifts, "lucky breaks"—while you feel stuck. That's not because Lakshmi favors them. It's because they've opened the channels, consciously or not. You can do the same.

Working with Lakshmi means creating a space where prosperity can land. You don't chase money. You don't beg the gods. You align. You clear space. You project your signal upward and outward—and then you invite her in with ritual and presence.

Most people in the west were never taught that money is a spiritual force. We were taught it's "just economics," or a necessary evil. But Lakshmi teaches something entirely different. Wealth is sacred. It's not about greed—it's about flow. When wealth flows through the right hands, it builds families, empowers healing, creates safety, and opens futures. When it stagnates or gets hoarded, it starts to decay the soul of the one clutching it.

Lakshmi's magik is precise. It tunes into your intentions. Are you asking for wealth to escape your life? She won't respond. Are you asking to express more, grow more, create more? Then she starts to move. Her current meets you halfway.

That's why in my rituals, I don't "petition" Lakshmi like a supplicant. I meet her like a co-creator. I set the space with beauty. I burn my favorite incense—Nag Champa from the 70s if I can get it. I light a gold or green candle, depending on the vibe. I speak clearly, not as if I'm groveling, but as if I'm welcoming an honored guest who I trust will bring only what matches my vibration.

Now here's the deeper current: Lakshmi doesn't only bring "cash." She brings opportunity. She brings the right person at the right time. She brings energy that clears out the blocks so your ideas can become income. You may ask for money and instead find yourself offered a business connection, a new job, or a creative surge that leads to success. That's her at work. It's not always instant, but when she moves, it's smooth. Elegant. And unmistakable.

Let's look at a myth that encodes this truth.

A Story That Encodes Her Power

In one of the oldest stories of creation, the gods and demons churned the cosmic ocean to retrieve treasures from the depths. This wasn't a casual act—it was a violent, drawn-out labor between opposing forces. From that ocean, many things emerged. But Lakshmi was the crown jewel.

She rose from the ocean seated on a lotus, glowing with power. And the gods were stunned. She embodied everything they'd lost: grace, abundance, fertility, and joy. Every being wanted her. She was the spark that could restore divine order.

But Lakshmi didn't pick the strongest. She didn't go to the one who demanded her. She chose Vishnu—the god of balance and preservation. That choice carries deep meaning.

She doesn't respond to force. She doesn't care for status. She flows to those who can hold her vibration with steadiness.

That's the secret encoded in the myth: Lakshmi chooses alignment, not power. She chooses presence over need.

And if you want her to stay in your life, you don't just summon her once. You live in a way that matches her frequency—calm, intentional, graceful.

The Rituals

From here, we move into the three core ritual types you can use to call in her wealth current. Each is built around a different need: fast cash, long-term growth, or career/business elevation. Each taps into a different facet of her magikal field.

But before you begin any of them—stop. Take some time to clean up your space. Light your incense. Take a breath and clear your mind. Don't carry your stress into the ritual like it's a customer service complaint.

Bring your best self, even if just for fifteen minutes.

Then the current can begin.

Quick Wealth: For Sudden Windfalls or Lucky Breaks

Use when you need fast results—unexpected money, a gift, a "lucky" twist.

Items Needed:

- Green or gold ritual candle
- A dollar bill or local currency note
- A small bowl of water
- Incense (Nag Champa or lotus)
- Offering: Sweet fruit or a bit of honey in water

Steps:

Light your incense and candle.

Place the bowl of water in front of Lakshmi's image, or yantra.

Speak aloud:

"Lakshmi, river of gold, shine fortune into my life. Let money come as a gift, as a surprise, as a flow that cannot be blocked."

Hold the money in your hands. Imagine it multiplying.

Dip the dollar's corner into the water and say:

"As water flows, let wealth come to me—unexpected, generous, joyful."

Thank her. Place the dollar under your pillow or in your wallet.

Variation:

Write your need on the bill. Burn a small piece in a fire-safe bowl and say:

"Gone from my hands, returned tenfold."

Offer a glass of wine or milk to seal the exchange.

Steady Wealth Accumulation

Use when building savings, growing investments, or laying long-term financial roots.

Items Needed:

- Brown or gold candle
- Sandalwood incense
- A small bowl of rice or coins
- Image or statue of Lakshmi

Steps:

Clean your altar space.

Light the incense and candle.

Place the rice or coins in a bowl.

Speak:

> *"Lakshmi, build me a house of wealth. Brick by brick, let abundance rise."*

Meditate on slow, steady growth—compound interest, rising profits, sustainable income.

Leave the bowl out overnight. Bury the rice in the earth or donate the coins next day.

Variation:

Repeat this ritual weekly with a new coin or grain added each time. You're feeding the flow.

Business Success & Career Prosperity

Best for career goals, landing clients, or boosting influence.

Items Needed:

- Yellow candle
- Cinnamon incense
- A business card or job application (or a handwritten summary of your goal)
- A coin (ANY coin)

Steps:

Set the paper or business card on the altar.

Light candle and incense.

Say:

"Lakshmi, walk with me into my success. Let the doors open, the calls come, the work arrive."

Circle the coin three times around the card, clockwise.

Offer the coin to her. Drop it into a special jar or box that only holds "Lakshmi coins."

Variation:

Keep the business card on your person for the next few days. Smudge it with cinnamon smoke each morning.

Lakshmi's Connection to Gold, Water & Prosperity Flows

Gold isn't just a symbol. It's a conductor.

It holds frequency. When used in ritual, even a fake gold

item can carry that imprint.

Water is her native element. She rose from it. She rides a lotus that grows in water.

So always have some water in her rituals—still or flowing.

If you place a gold coin in a glass of spring water under the moonlight, you create a simple but powerful energy battery that holds her current. Keep that water near your wallet, your desk, or your altar, and refresh it every few days. There's no need to chase or beg—just prepare the field. She'll come.

CHAPTER 7

Family Magik

Wealth, Harmony, and the Magik of the Household

In every Hindu home, there's an altar, a photo, or at least a whisper of her name. Lakshmi—the *Grihalakshmi*—the radiant queen who rules not from a temple, but from within the walls of the home itself. She's not distant. She doesn't live in the heavens. She lives in the kitchen, in the bank account, in the warmth between family members, in the silence after an argument, and in the birth of a child.

Traditionally, Grihalakshmi is the aspect of Lakshmi that blesses the household. She isn't only about money. She's about stability. Peace. Flow. She ensures the family stays fed, bonded, and growing. Her presence is the subtle golden thread running through generations, tying the past and future together. She blesses the daughter-in-law who cooks, the father who provides, the child who learns, and the grandmother who watches it all.

She doesn't just bring in the money. She helps you keep it. She prevents waste, loss, and chaos. Her blessing is felt when you wake up and feel settled. Not rich—but held. That's her current.

This aspect of her has been honored in kitchens and courtyards for thousands of years. Not with fancy rites, but with the smell of incense before breakfast. The offering of the first scoop of rice. The bowl of milk left quietly in the corner of the house. In these small acts, Lakshmi is called—not for power, but for presence.

And here's where it changes for us.

In modern magik, we often chase wealth like it's a separate force. Like we can force it to appear through will alone. But if your home is misaligned—if your field is filled with noise, pain, or resentment—it repels the current Lakshmi brings. You can manifest all day, but it leaks out the back door.

This chapter is about fixing that leak.

When I began reworking my own systems, Lakshmi's energy kept returning to one thing: the family field. Most wealth blocks don't start with us. They're inherited. Not just through trauma, but through energy design. Emotional patterns. Beliefs handed down. Guilt passed off like heirlooms.

Some families pass down land. Others pass down shame.

That's what we're going to rewire. You'll work directly with Lakshmi to purify the emotional wiring of the household. You'll clear old stories, open stuck doors, and rebuild the home's energetic map. You'll speak to her not as a goddess in the sky—but as the silent witness standing behind you at the kitchen sink, waiting for you to notice she's already there.

My methods don't replace tradition. They activate it. They take the old current and fuse it with conscious intent. You're not just inviting Lakshmi into your home. You're turning her into a full partner in its operation.

Family magik isn't about making people behave. It's about shaping the field so that peace is easier than war. So that money stays longer. So that blessings land where they're meant to—and don't get lost in the noise.

This is where Lakshmi lives. And this is where we begin.

Harmony in the Home

Lakshmi won't stay in a house where there's constant bickering, tension, or cruelty. You might draw her in with offerings—but she'll leave if the space turns toxic.

This ritual is for smoothing out the static. Arguments that repeat. Siblings who don't speak. Parents who don't listen. You're not "fixing" anyone—you're cleaning the energetic house. Lakshmi enters once the field is calm enough to hold her.

This isn't a love-and-light spell. It's a reset button. It breaks the echo. After this ritual, you'll notice a pause before old patterns kick in. That pause is your opening. That's where the healing begins.

Items Needed
- White candle (or pink, if available)
- Nag Champa incense
- Small bowl of milk or sweetened tea (as offering)

Steps
Light your candle and incense. Sit in the center of your home or near the family room.

Say: *"Lakshmi, Grihalakshmi, bring peace to this house. Calm the echoes. Reset the field."*

Visualize a wave of golden energy moving through the home, touching each room and clearing static.

Place the offering near the candle. Say: *"This is for you. Bring calm, bring warmth, bring unity."*

Let the candle burn for at least 15 minutes. Snuff it out when done. Leave the offering until the next morning.

Repeat weekly if needed, especially after conflict.

Domestic Success
This ritual is for activating the household engine—daily life, chores, bills, teamwork, rhythms. Think of it as running a shop. Every person plays a role. When the gears grind, things break down—missed payments, broken appliances, tension in

the walls.

Lakshmi thrives in flow. This ritual charges the energy of the home as an entity, not just a shelter. It turns your living space into a living system. You'll find ease in the day-to-day. Cooking becomes sacred. Bills are paid with grace. Rooms feel alive again.

Do this when you feel the house is "off" but can't put your finger on it.

Items Needed

- Yellow candle (or white)
- Nag Champa incense
- A few coins or a spoon of uncooked rice (as offering)

Steps

Light your candle and incense. Stand near your kitchen or workspace.

Say: *"Lakshmi, light of the home, make this space function with grace and flow."*

Walk through the house slowly, visualizing golden gears turning and oiling the parts of daily life—cleaning, paying bills, working, sleeping.

Set the offering by the front door or hearth. Say: *"I give this with gratitude. Let this home be blessed and whole."*

Leave the coins or rice overnight. Dispose the next day by giving it to nature or placing it in a planter.

Intergenerational Wealth Flow

If your parents struggled, you likely inherited it—not just in money, but in programming. This ritual is about opening the pipeline between ancestors, yourself, and future generations. Think of it as healing the flow of wealth across time.

Lakshmi responds when the energy is directed both forward and backward. You thank those who came before, clear their mistakes, and plant new patterns for those who come after. It's more than manifesting money—it's declaring that your family line is no longer a site of lack.

This ritual is potent when paired with physical actions—investing, buying land, creating trusts, even just opening a bank account for your child. You become the wealth anchor. Lakshmi responds to that commitment.

Wealth Line Ritual
Items Needed

- Green candle (or white)
- Nag Champa incense
- A photo or written names of ancestors and future children (even if not yet born)
- Small bowl of honey or fruit (as offering)

Steps

Light the candle and incense. Set out the photos or names

in front of you.

Say: *"Lakshmi, I speak across time. Heal the wounds behind me. Bless the ones ahead."*

Imagine a golden stream flowing from behind your back, through your spine, and into the future.

Place the offering next to the candle. Say: *"I open the river of wealth in my name and theirs."*

Leave the candle burning 15 minutes. Leave the offering for 24 hours, then bury or pour outside.

Preventing Financial Misfortune in Family Lines

Some families carry a curse. Not one cast with bones or blood—but a chain of bad decisions, self-sabotage, addiction, poverty mindsets. You see it over and over: job losses, inheritance wasted, businesses collapsing.

This ritual is for cutting that line. You don't banish a demon—you erase the code. Lakshmi steps in as a firewall. She doesn't just bring wealth—she guards it.

You'll be working with her protective aspects here. The ones that see everything, even before it happens. This ritual is part shield, part reprogramming. Once done, the bad luck will start to miss your family.

Ritual to Break the Chain

Items Needed

- Black candle (or white)
- Nag Champa incense
- A piece of thread or string
- Small glass of clean water (as offering)

Steps

Light your candle and incense. Hold the thread in both hands.

Say: *"Lakshmi, guardian of the line, I cut what does not belong. Misfortune ends with me."*

Visualize the thread representing the curse or inherited pattern. Break it deliberately.

Place the thread under the candle, and the water beside it.

Say: *"Cleanse the past. Seal the future."*

Let the candle burn down. Pour the water outside. Dispose of the thread by either burning or burying it.

Safe Conception & Birth Ritual

Most don't think of Lakshmi when they think of childbirth. But in South Indian traditions, she's one of the three goddesses called upon during labor—Lakshmi, Parvati, and Saraswati. Lakshmi brings ease to the body, prosperity to the womb, and a safe journey for the child.

If you're trying to conceive, or know someone who is, her energy can be gently woven into that process. She blesses not only the baby—but the home the baby will enter. Her energy says: this child will be provided for.

This is a quiet ritual. It doesn't shout. But its power runs deep, especially when there's been trauma, loss, or difficulty in past pregnancies.

She holds space, and that space becomes life.

Conception & Safe Birth Ritual

Items Needed

- Light blue or white candle
- Nag Champa incense
- A glass of milk or a sweet (as offering)

Steps

Light the candle and incense in a peaceful space. Sit quietly with your hand over your womb or belly.

Say: *"Lakshmi, gentle mother, bless the path for this child. Bring peace to the gate of life."*

Visualize soft golden light filling your body and the space around you.

Place the offering beside you. Say: *"For the soul waiting to arrive, may they be met with love and wealth."*

Repeat weekly or before conception attempts. Leave the offering until morning.

CHAPTER 8

Lakshmi's Connection to Love & Sex Magik

Love isn't just soft whispers and sweet words. It's power. And like wealth, love can be summoned, shaped, and anchored. Lakshmi holds that power in her hands—not in the way a Western magician might expect, but in the way a river holds a current. Effortless, constant, and able to shape mountains.

She is known as the Goddess of Fortune, but what's often missed is that fortune isn't only gold. It's connection. Beauty. Companionship. Sexual energy that flows like honey and fire. In Vedic tradition, Lakshmi's name itself contains the root laksya—meaning "aim" or "goal." And the aim of love, whether it's erotic, romantic, or soul-deep, is fulfillment. Satisfaction. Abundance in the form of another being who reflects our joy back to us.

In the old stories, Lakshmi rises from the cosmic ocean,

born not of death but of divine churn. She chooses Vishnu as her consort not out of submission, but because she wants him. He mirrors her peace, her wisdom, her strength. It's not a story of rescue. It's a story of resonance. She brings grace to his power. She softens his edges, while he gives her form in the world. Together, they represent a model of divine partnership—mutual magnetism without domination.

That's the energy you call on in her love and sex magik.

It's not Aphrodite's raw seduction, or Venus's social charm. Lakshmi's love magik doesn't burn hot and quick—it coils like silk around your aura and draws others in. She doesn't push. She pulls. She makes you beautiful to others, not by changing your appearance, but by amplifying your frequency. Under her gaze, people want to be near you. They want to help. They want to please you.

This is love as magnetism.

Let's break that into ritual types so you can see how this works in your life.

First is attraction. Not just for romance, but for anything you want to draw into your orbit. A lover. A business partner. An ally. Lakshmi makes your energy warm and irresistible. People notice you. They linger. You don't chase. They offer. Her aura blends glamour with grace—like walking into a room and making heads turn, not because you're flashy, but because you radiate something they want to be near.

Then there's sexuality—not raunchy chaos, but divine sensuality. This is where she's often misunderstood. Lakshmi doesn't shy away from sexual energy. She wields it. In Tantra, she is Shakti, the active life-force. When you call on her for sex magik, the goal isn't just orgasm. It's energetic fusion. Intentional climax. You imprint your will at the moment of peak ecstasy and send it echoing into the world. You don't drain energy—you create it. The body becomes a temple, the act becomes a spell.

Next is emotional bonding. Strengthening the tie between two souls, or healing where something broke. Lakshmi doesn't do rage or revenge—that's Kali's domain. She builds connection. Trust. Loyalty. You can call her into a relationship to remove jealousy, to increase affection, or to help both people remember why they chose each other in the first place. She's the calm after the storm. The hand that reaches out and says, Let's begin again.

Then there's wealth in relationships. This is subtle, but it's one of her strongest powers. A relationship can be poor even with money flowing. Or it can be rich in laughter, growth, and shared dreams. Lakshmi tunes your connections to support abundance. That can mean attracting a lover who improves your fortunes. Or a partner who helps you rise, rather than dragging you down. She will clean house energetically. If someone is draining you, she will shift the field until either they rise to meet you, or they fall away. It's not always gentle—but it's always aligned.

Now let's bring in the comparison with Venus and Aphrodite.

Aphrodite is fire. She's lust, raw emotion, jealousy, beauty weaponized. She starts wars. She inspires poets. Her love is tumultuous, intoxicating, and rarely stable.

Venus, in Roman myth, is a bit softer—social charm, fertility, diplomacy. She's still powerful, but more strategic. She works the court. She plays the game.

Lakshmi is different. She doesn't seduce. She doesn't manipulate. She simply is, and people move toward her. Her presence activates love, wealth, and desire without effort. No need for elaborate games or power struggles. If you align with her, your energy becomes the invitation.

You don't have to convince anyone to love you. They already feel like they do.

That's the difference. That's the magik.

She shows you how to become the source of the thing you want. And when you become that source—whether it's joy, affection, magnetism, or abundance—others naturally reflect it back.

That's how you begin to shift your field with her rituals.

Use white candles if you don't have red or pink. Use Nag Champa or any sweet, floral incense. Offer honey, rose petals, a splash of perfume—anything that smells beautiful and feels sensual. Keep it grounded. Keep it clear. Keep it honest.

This isn't about casting a net. It's about shining like a lighthouse.

Let's begin.

Attraction & Magnetism

To amplify your aura and draw romantic attention, allies, or general admiration.

Items

- White candle (pink/red optional)
- Nag Champa/floral incense
- small mirror
- offering of honey or flower.

Steps:

Energize your space with intention.

Light candle and incense. Face mirror.

Say: *"Lakshmi, who draws all beauty and joy, shine through me now..."*

Gaze into the mirror. Visualize a glow.

Offer honey/flower. Say: *"May sweetness pour from me..."*

Snuff candle or let burn safely.

Sexual Energy & Magnetic Desire

To awaken sensual force and channel it into confidence and desire.

Items:

- White/red candle
- sensual incense (jasmine/rose)

- perfume or spice (clove/cardamom)

Steps:

Move or stretch to activate your body.

Light candle and incense.

Say: *"Lakshmi, sacred current of desire, awaken in me…"*

Visualize spiral of red-orange light rising through you.

Offer perfume/spice. Whisper: *"From sweetness to fire…"*

Snuff candle after working.

Strengthening Emotional Bonds

To increase affection and repair emotional ties.

Items

- White candle
- lavender incense
- sweet fruit or food

Steps:

Focus on the person you wish to bond with.

Light candle and incense.

Say: *"Lakshmi of union and peace, smooth the path between us…"*

Imagine a pink-gold thread between your hearts.

Offer sweetness. Say: *"Let our bond be fed…"*

Snuff candle. Speak a message if you wish.

Wealth in Love & Relationships

To call in or upgrade a relationship that supports prosperity.

Items:

- White/gold candle
- Sandalwood incense
- Coin, or a crystal or jewelry.

Steps:

Clarify your intention.

Light candle and incense.

Say: *"Lakshmi, who blesses unions with gold and growth..."*

Charge offering with your vision.

Offer the item. Say: *"What I give in love returns to me..."*

Snuff candle.

Bonus Ritual – Healing from Heartbreak

Purpose: To release grief and reclaim your energy.

Items

- White candle
- lavender incense
- bowl of water or tear-shaped stone.

Steps:

Sit quietly. Allow the pain to be seen.

Light candle and incense.

Say: *"Lakshmi, who holds the ocean of love, gather the pieces of my heart…"*

Place hands on chest. Breathe.

Offer water/stone. Whisper: *"I release what was…"*

Snuff candle. Pour water outside or return stone to earth.

2nd Bonus Ritual – Rekindling Sexual Spark

Purpose: To reawaken desire within yourself or with a partner.

Items

- White/red candle
- rose incense
- rose petal or chocolate offerings

Steps:

Light candle and incense.

Say: *"Lakshmi, flowing joy of the body, awaken warmth where it cooled…"*

Imagine warmth rising through your chest.

Offer sensual item. Say: *"I invite delight back into the dance."*

Share or enjoy the offering slowly.

Let energy carry into your next moment.

Love is wealth. Desire is current. Lakshmi shows you how to receive both—without shame, without chase, without apology.

CHAPTER 9

Love and Sexuality: Lakshmi's Hidden Power

Lakshmi isn't all coins and lotus flowers. She's also the heat in the body, the glow in the skin, the spark between lovers.

Magicians often forget that love is a form of wealth. Relationships, attraction, pleasure, intimacy—these are currencies. And Lakshmi rules them just as surely as she rules gold.

When her energy flows in your life, you become magnetic. You attract people, not just romantically, but socially, emotionally, spiritually. You draw in allies, clients, friends, and lovers. You shine. People don't know why they want to be around you—but they do. That's her touch.

Her love energy is subtle. It doesn't blast through your life like Venus might, shaking beds and throwing flower petals. Lakshmi works quieter. She oils the wheels of desire. She stirs affection. She deepens bonds that already exist and gently dissolves those that block your flow.

Here's where she differs from Venus or Aphrodite.

Those spirits ignite. They seduce. They heighten the moment.

Lakshmi sustains. She strengthens the thread.

Aphrodite brings a lover into your bed. Lakshmi helps them stay. She's not a seductress. She's a keeper of love's hearth. She blesses committed bonds and teaches us to value love that builds. When you call on her for attraction, don't expect chaos. Expect a slow, building flame.

But yes—she can stir lust, too. She is not shy. She's not a nun. She loves adornment, dance, beauty, fragrance, and indulgence. Sex isn't shameful under her gaze—it's sacred. A way to transmit energy, to fuse, to exchange abundance through bodies.

When love stagnates or intimacy fades, that's a sign of blocked Lakshmi flow. She doesn't just draw love in—she keeps it alive. Think of her like warm oil in the lamp. Without it, the light dims. With her, it stays lit.

That's the principle behind this work: to restore flow in your love life by calling her into the energy field. She clears the block, then calls in the match.

Let's get to the rituals.

Ritual 1: Attraction and Magnetism

Draw a compatible lover or romantic opportunity into your life.

Items Needed:

- One pink or white candle
- Nag Champa or rose incense
- A small mirror
- A piece of rose quartz
- A drop of perfume or scented oil you like

Steps:

Clean your space and body.

Light the candle and incense.

Gaze into the mirror. Say aloud:

"I see beauty. I see love. Lakshmi, light me up from within."

Rub the perfume lightly on your neck and heart.

Hold the rose quartz. Imagine your body glowing pink, radiant and attractive.

Whisper your desire to Lakshmi.

Let the candle burn for at least 9 minutes.

Thank her, close the space, and keep the mirror near your bed.

Ritual 2: Strengthen Bonds and Emotional Intimacy

Goal: Deepen love with an existing partner or stabilize a relationship going through stress.

Items Needed:

- Two white candles
- A cup of sweet tea or warm milk
- Two strands of red thread or yarn
- One photo of you and the person (optional)

Steps:

Light both candles and place them close together.

Lay the red threads between them, tying the ends if you can.

Sip the sweet tea or milk and say:

"Let sweetness fill our bond. Let love return."

Place your hands over the photo or just focus on the person.

Call Lakshmi:

"Goddess of grace, bless this love. Heal what's wounded. Deepen what's strong."

Imagine the threads pulsing with red light.

When ready, tie them together and keep them in a safe place.

Let candles burn out naturally or snuff gently.

CHAPTER 10

Control Over Fate & Destiny
Lakshmi and the Karmic Web

Fate isn't fixed, and destiny isn't some divine lottery ticket drawn by chance. It's shaped, constantly—through your choices, your thoughts, the energy you carry, and the actions you repeat. Every moment becomes part of a larger pattern, a ripple in the karmic field, looping through time until it's resolved, released, or rewritten.

Karma is often misunderstood. It's not some punishment system or a cosmic slap for being human. It's a structure. It's code. It's energetic math that responds to how you move through this life—and the ones before. And Lakshmi doesn't judge it. She guides it. She adjusts the flow. She offers tools for you to work with it, untangle it, and redirect it. That's the deeper level of her power, the one that moves far beyond money or luck. It's the aspect of her that rethreads your storyline from the inside out.

If you've felt stuck—trapped in cycles you can't explain, constantly pulled back to the same point no matter how hard you push forward—there's a good chance it's karmic. You're not being blocked for no reason. Something old is playing out. Sometimes it's yours. Sometimes it's ancestral. But the end result is the same: you're locked into a script that no longer fits who you are becoming. That's where this work begins.

When you bring offerings to Lakshmi—not as bribes, but as signals—you're telling the pattern it's time to shift. When you light a candle with intention, speak the truth aloud, or cut energetic cords, you're taking conscious control of unconscious cycles. This is how you stop reacting to fate and start shaping it. Ritual becomes the tool, Lakshmi the ally, and your own will the flame that initiates the reset.

Lakshmi holds sway over cycles of birth and rebirth—not just physical lives, but the patterns within a life that keep repeating. She's the goddess who offers renewal through beauty, through grace, through gold—but behind that grace is precision. If you've lived through chaos, if your family line is soaked in generational pain, or if you've simply had enough of the same walls rising in your path, this is the place to shift that frequency.

We'll begin this chapter with karmic correction: ritual offerings and reprogramming to clear the blocks that bind you to outdated energy. Then we'll go deeper—cutting karmic ties to people, dissolving money-related karmic scars, and anchoring your fate to a new stream of luck and abundance. Finally, you'll ask Lakshmi to reveal the path ahead, the one that actually works, the one you may have overlooked or forgotten.

That final ritual is designed to lead directly into the Pathworking chapter later in the book. It opens your awareness, tunes your inner compass, and prepares your spirit to recognize the markers Lakshmi sets on your road.

This is how you take back authorship of your own story.

Let's begin.

Karmic Offering to Shift Stagnant Fate

Reset the energy of past karma by offering a symbolic trade to Lakshmi.

Items Needed:

- Blue or violet candle (White if unavailable)
- Incense (Nag Champa or similar)
- Small bowl of milk or plain cooked rice
- A single coin (any denomination)

Steps:

Light the candle and incense. Sit with the coin in your hand.

Say aloud:

"Lakshmi, I offer this token in place of what binds me. Rewrite the pattern. Clear the debt.

Shift the weight that stalls my path."

Place the coin next to the bowl. Leave both on your altar or windowsill for one night.

The next morning, bury the coin at the base of a healthy plant or tree. Dispose of the offering in running water or in the earth.

Cutting Karmic Bonds with Others

Break unhealthy karmic ties to people who are holding you back.

Items Needed:

- Black or deep indigo candle (White if unavailable)
- Incense
- A short piece of string or thread
- Small bowl of saltwater
- A slip of paper

Steps:

Write their full name on the paper.

Tie a single knot in the string while thinking of the energetic pull they have on you.

Light the candle and say:

"Lakshmi, guide of cycles,

let this knot be undone.

Let their path be theirs, mine be mine."

Burn the string safely. Drop the paper into the saltwater.

After the candle burns for a while, pour the saltwater out

away from your home.

Clearing Karmic Poverty Codes

Dissolve inherited fears, lack-mindsets, and guilt around money.

Items Needed:

- Green or gold candle (White if unavailable)
- Incense
- A small bowl of honey
- One coin or bill (can be symbolic)

Steps:

Dab the coin or bill with a bit of honey.

Light the candle and hold the coin in your palm.

Say:

"Lakshmi, reset this code.

Melt the memory of lack.

Open flow. Rewrite my wealth."

Place the honeyed coin on the altar overnight.

In the morning, keep the coin with you for seven days—or give it away to someone in need.

Anchoring a New Karmic Stream (Future Flow)

Embed a new karmic timeline aligned with clarity, flow, and higher wealth.

Items Needed:

- Gold or white candle
- Incense
- A small charm, stone, or item that can be carried
- Thread (white, gold, or any light color)

Steps:

Wrap the charm loosely in the thread.

Light the candle and say:

"Lakshmi, align me to the higher stream.

I step into the future written in gold.

Anchor me in fortune that flows true."

Let the charm sit by the candle for at least 15 minutes.

Unwrap it and carry it on you daily.

Revelation of the Path to Success

Ask Lakshmi to reveal the strongest personal path to abundance and alignment.

Items Needed:

- White or pale yellow candle
- Incense
- Clear glass of water
- Journal or blank page

Steps:

Light the candle and incense. Set the water in front of you.

Gaze into the water and speak:

"Lakshmi, revealer of paths, open my sight.

Show me the door that waits.

Let my feet find what my mind cannot."

Watch the surface of the water. Let images, words, or memories rise.

Write anything that comes into your journal—no filtering.

Close with:

"I accept your signs. I will follow."

All five rituals tie directly into her karmic rebalancing power. The last ritual sets you up for deeper work in the Pathworking chapter.

CHAPTER 11

Guardian of Cosmic Order (Ṛta)

You can hustle. You can chant mantras. You can throw every ritual in the book at your money problems. But if you're out of alignment with Ṛta, it won't stick. It slips through your hands like water. Ṛta is cosmic order. Not rules or morality— harmony. It's the original frequency. The underlying structure that makes everything else work. When things click, when life flows and your efforts bear fruit, that's Ṛta. When there's resistance, chaos, or repeated setbacks, it's a sign that you're misaligned.

Most people haven't heard of Ṛta, and even in spiritual circles it's often buried beneath more familiar terms like karma or dharma. But Ṛta is older than both. It's what karma and dharma are built on. Without it, they don't function. Ṛta is the natural law that governs balance, rightness, and flow. It doesn't judge. It doesn't punish. It just is. And Lakshmi isn't just a symbol of prosperity. She's the pulse that flows through aligned systems. She appears when Ṛta is upheld. She disappears when it's broken.

In the Vedas, kings who ruled with justice were said to attract Lakshmi. Crops grew. The land flourished. People thrived. But when those same kings became greedy or unjust, Lakshmi vanished. It wasn't a curse. It was cause and effect. She is not a reward. She is alignment, made visible. And she will not remain in places where the current of truth has stopped flowing.

So what does this mean in your actual life? It means wealth, luck, and opportunities aren't just about effort. They're about timing, harmony, and being in tune with that cosmic current. When you are, things fall into place without strain. When you're not, even the best plans fall apart. Alignment with Ṛta isn't perfection. It's truth. It's the willingness to correct what needs correcting, even if no one else sees it.

You may feel like you're doing everything right and still struggling. You meditate, visualize, burn the candles. But if you're lying to yourself, avoiding action, or clinging to things that no longer serve, then Lakshmi has likely stepped back. Not as punishment. Just as response. Her flow doesn't tolerate distortion.

Violating Ṛta doesn't always look dramatic. It's often subtle. It's the business deal you know isn't fair, but take anyway. The lie you tell to make something easier. The instinct you ignore. Over time, these small misalignments stack. Then the flow slows. The luck runs dry. You burn out. That's not failure. That's the signal to stop and reset.

When you're in sync with Ṛta, you don't have to chase. The clients call you. The money arrives early. The right people cross your path at just the right time. Synchronicity becomes normal. You feel stable, even in movement. There is a rhythm to your days. That's not coincidence. That's cosmic order responding to your field.

Lakshmi follows the hum of Ṛta. She rides that frequency like a wave. When your life hits that harmonic, she arrives. That's when doors open. That's when you wake up feeling like something has shifted. And if you're paying attention, you'll catch those moments—the strange timing of a call, the chance meeting, the way everything just lines up.

When Ṛta is broken, you'll feel it. The energy gets weird. You start second-guessing everything. Deals stall, messages get lost, health issues pop up. It's not always immediate, but the signal is clear. Something's out of tune. It's not personal. It's energetic. Ṛta is a system-level current, not a cosmic personality. But Lakshmi is the presence that tells you whether you're still in the flow.

There are stories of Lakshmi testing people. Not with trials, but with truth. She watches how you treat others when no one's looking. How you spend your money. Whether you give when it's inconvenient. Whether your wealth makes others' lives better, or worse. Her presence magnifies what's already there. If you're in tune with Ṛta, she lifts you higher. If you're not, she doesn't punish you—she just vanishes.

I've seen this in my own life. There were times when I was working nonstop and still felt like everything was slipping. It wasn't the effort that was wrong—it was the direction. I was ignoring what I knew needed to shift. The moment I made that shift, the flow came back. Calls returned. Payments cleared. That's not coincidence. That's a realignment. And that's her.

You don't need a priest or a temple to access Ṛta. You just need to stop pretending you don't know what's wrong. You do. That little knot in your gut? That hesitation you've been brushing off? That's your signal. Honor it. Fix what you can. The rest will open up.

Lakshmi Ritual to Restore Ṛta
Items Needed:

- White candle
- Incense (Nag Champa or similar)
- A coin (silver or gold-tone)
- A glass of water (to represent purity and flow)

Steps:

Light the candle and incense. Breathe. Settle your energy.

Place the coin in front of the candle. Say: *"Lakshmi, guardian of Ṛta, I restore what was broken. I honor the flow. Return to me with your grace."*

Place your hands over the water. Visualize it filling with clarity.

Speak your truth aloud—what you're now ready to fix, own, or release.

Leave the coin on your altar overnight. Pour the water into a plant or clean ground the next day.

Thank her. Then act on what you just spoke.

You can repeat this ritual once a week until you feel her presence return. It's not about pleasing her. It's about restoring the current she rides. If you're truthful, she comes.

You can also build a longer practice around Ṛta. Keep a small notebook titled "Alignments." Every day, write down one thing you did to restore order. It can be tiny: fixing a broken drawer, telling someone the truth, honoring a promise. Over time, these acts build momentum.

Lakshmi is drawn to people who carry order in their field. Not control. Not perfection. Just honest, living order. She shows up for those who respect the flow and contribute to it. And when she shows up, everything changes.

Don't just perform the ritual. Live it. Ṛta doesn't care about performances. It responds to reality. And so does Lakshmi. She is not far. She's just waiting for truth to open the door.

CHAPTER 12

Pathworking Lakshmi
Direct Contact Through Inner Vision

You don't need a chant. You don't need incense or a room full of candles. Though those things can help set the mood, they're not required. What you need is alignment—your energy, your intent, and your focus. That's how we contact Lakshmi. That's how we shift from hoping she hears us to knowing we've reached her. This chapter is about stepping beyond ritual and into raw, direct energy contact. No tools. No scripts. Just you and her.

We've already gone through traditional offerings, mantras, and altar setups. All of that builds a current, yes— but once you've tapped into her frequency, you don't always need the physical layers. This is where we begin introducing a more subtle approach. What magicians call pathworking is really just inner travel, a form of focused vision that leads to energetic contact. It's meditation, but deeper. You're not just relaxing—you're moving.

You're going somewhere.

And I'll be straight with you—this isn't theory. I've done it. For years, I worked with gods, spirits, and forces the old way. Candle. Incense. Circle. Spoken word. But something shifted once I started using pathworking. It started simple. I'd visualize a deity's symbol. Or a temple. Or a scene from their mythology. I'd sit with it long enough until something clicked. A shift in energy. A presence. The sense of being watched back. That's when I realized I wasn't just "seeing" them. I was meeting them.

It happened with Lakshmi one night when I was using the simplest visualization—just a golden lotus floating on water. I focused on it. Let it rise in my mind. And then the scene built itself. The lotus grew large enough to stand on. Stars above. Ocean below. The wind carried incense I never lit. That's when she stepped into view—not from the image, but from behind it. From somewhere real. She didn't speak, not then. She just looked—and I knew something permanent had shifted.

After that, I stopped worrying about "proper" meditation. I started using astral travel. Not the kind where you fight to leave your body and float like a ghost. No. This was smoother. Cleaner. Like stepping sideways through a doorway that had always been there. I'd start with pathworking—get into the scene—and if I stayed there long enough, the vision became stable. My energy body would just move into the scene. The shift was unmistakable. You're no longer watching the scene—you're in it.

This method made contact easier. And stronger. And it doesn't just work with Lakshmi. But she's one of the best to start with. Her energy is welcoming. Calm. Deeply powerful, but not overwhelming. She wants connection. And when you reach out, she'll meet you halfway.

This is what I mean by alignment. The symbols, the colors, the visual scenes—they tune your frequency. Like turning a radio dial until the static clears. You don't have to get it perfect. Just consistent. If you show up with truth in your chest, she shows up in hers.

Now, don't get stuck thinking you have to "see" her clearly. This isn't about how vivid your mental picture is. Some people feel her first. A pressure in the room. A rush of warmth through the ribs. Some hear her voice like a thought that didn't come from them. Others just know something changed. You'll find your way.

This is where magik becomes lived experience. You don't just read about Lakshmi. You meet her. You ask her questions. You feel her reply. Sometimes in words, sometimes in sensation, sometimes in the way your life tilts afterward. The key is presence. Focus. And repetition. Show up enough, and you'll start walking her world like it's your own.

Before we step into the pathworking itself, take a moment

to feel what kind of entry point draws you. Some magicians are drawn to temples—vast marble halls filled with light and quiet power. Others find their way through the ocean, floating on a golden lotus under a night sky. Some are carried by starlight, some by music, some by fire. Let it come naturally. Don't try to force the setting. If you see her seated beside Vishnu in a jewel-studded palace, that's valid. If she meets you barefoot in a garden, that's valid too. What matters is the feeling—the charge in the air when you're close.

Over time, your personal gateway may change. That's fine. Each path is a reflection of your current alignment. Don't worry if it doesn't look like someone else's. What works is what brings you into her presence. Trust your path.

Let's walk it together.

Step-by-Step Pathworking to Lakshmi

Step 1: Set Your Intention
Speak it aloud or silently.

"I come to meet Lakshmi. I ask to know her energy and receive her guidance."

Say it with truth. Say it like you mean it.

Step 2: Breathe and Drop In
Close your eyes.

Breathe slow and deep. In through the nose. Out through the mouth.

On each exhale, release tension. Drop your shoulders.

Let the world go dim. Let your body get heavy.

Keep breathing until your thoughts start to drift.

Step 3: Build the Vision

See a golden lotus floating in space.

Or see the ocean, still and shining under stars.

Or see a great temple glowing with soft, rose-colored light.

Choose one—whichever comes easiest. Go with it.

You're walking toward it. Every step, your energy lightens.

Step 4: Enter Her Space

If you chose the temple, walk up the steps and go inside.

If it's the ocean, let a wave rise and lift you.

If it's the lotus, sit on it and feel it carry you upward.

You're now entering her domain.

Let it form around you. Don't force details. Let them emerge.

You may hear bells. Smell sandalwood. Feel a gentle warmth across your chest.

You're not making it up. That's her energy syncing with yours.

Step 5: Meet Lakshmi

She may look like the statues, or she may appear younger,

older, more cosmic, more human.

Trust what you see.

Let her eyes meet yours.

Say nothing at first. Just receive.

Feel what she sends. A word. A light. A flood of peace.

Let it settle in.

Step 6: Ask

Once you feel connected, ask your question.

Keep it simple. Keep it honest.

"What do I need to know right now?"

"How can I clear my path to wealth?"

"What do you want me to see?"

Listen with your body, not just your ears.

Her answers can be symbols, images, a sudden emotion.

Don't analyze. Just receive.

Step 7: Anchor and Return

When it feels complete, thank her.

Say it out loud in the vision: "Thank you, Lakshmi."

Then step back.

Let the image fade. Let the room you're in return to view.

Wiggle your fingers. Breathe deep.

Touch the ground or floor. Ground yourself.

Then write it down. Everything. Every flicker of light. Every word or vision.

Optional Deepening: Direct Astral Arrival in Lakshmi's Domain

Once you've practiced the first pathworking and built enough inner stillness, you may find that you don't need to "walk" in anymore. You can just arrive.

This variation is a direct method. No symbolic build-up. No layered scene. Just presence and projection.

Try this after the regular pathworking has become second nature.

1. Set the Command

Close your eyes.

Speak the intent with clarity:

"I now arrive in the domain of Lakshmi. Take me to her."

2. Drop Fast Into Theta

Use three deep breaths.

On each breath, count backward:

"Three." Inhale.

"Two." Exhale.

"One." Drop.

Now hold the breath for a moment, let your body vanish from focus. You're just awareness now. Floating.

3. Let the Light Pull You

Feel a golden-pink light start to glow in front of you. It doesn't blind. It draws.

Let it expand until it surrounds you.

Then lean into it. Fall forward. No resistance. No visuals needed yet.

4. Arrival

You'll feel the shift.

The scene may form around you without effort. It could be a glowing temple. A lotus-filled lake. A space of stars and silk and stillness.

Wherever you land, that's her space.

Not imagination—projection.

5. Acknowledge and Wait

You may feel her before you see her.

Let her arrive on her terms.

This isn't a conjuring—it's a visit. Be present. Be still.

If she appears, acknowledge her. Bow your head, if it feels right. Open your energy and let her meet you. You don't need to say anything yet. She already knows.

6. Let It Unfold

You might receive images. A gesture. A look.

You may be guided to walk with her. Or just sit in silence. Let it unfold.

7. Return With Grace

When it feels done, speak your gratitude aloud or in

thought.

"I thank you, Lakshmi. I will return."

Feel your energy pull gently back into your body.

Anchor by touching your hands together or placing them on your chest.

Then open your eyes.

You've now crossed into direct contact. Not once, but at will.

Use it when needed. Call on her when guidance, clarity, or alignment is missing.

She doesn't ask for perfection—only presence. Show up, and she will too.

APPENDIX

Ritual Tools & Substitutions

You don't need a temple or a suitcase full of crystals. You just need consistency, sincerity, and a few simple tools.

Common Items You'll Use

- **White candle**

  Use this as a universal substitute for any other ritual color. If you *can* find gold, pink, red, or green, great. But white always works.

- **Incense**

  Stick to **Nag Champa** if you can. It's sacred, widely available, and carries the right frequency.

  Substitutes: any natural sandalwood or rose incense.

- **Offering bowl or cup**

  For wine, water, or milk. Glass, clay, or brass preferred. Avoid plastic.

- **Flowers**

Preferably **lotus**, **rose**, or **marigold**.

If you can't find those, any fresh flower will work. No synthetic ones.

- **Coins or money**

  Use clean, shiny coins or currency as a symbol of wealth. Don't stress the denomination. A penny can channel as much as a hundred-dollar bill.

- **Journal or paper**

  For writing your requests, affirmations, or symbols.

- **Small mirror**

  Optional, but powerful for reflection magik and seeing Lakshmi's light within yourself.

Common Mistakes & How to Fix Them

Let's be real. Life happens. The ritual doesn't always go as planned. Here's what to do when things go sideways—without losing the flow.

Missed a day of your ritual cycle?

Don't panic. Lakshmi doesn't run on guilt. Just pick up where you left off. No need to restart the whole thing unless you feel it. The intent matters more than the calendar.

Candle blew out mid-ritual?

Relight it. Whisper, "Let this continue," and move on. If it keeps blowing out, check your space. Energy might be unstable. Ground yourself and try again.

You used the wrong color?

It's fine. White covers all bases. Lakshmi isn't judging your candle stash. She's tuning in to your heart, not your shopping list.

You forgot to give the offering?

Make it up the next day. Or, hold it in your hand, offer it silently, and place it on your altar later. It's about the connection, not the timing.

Incense ran out?

Burn something natural if you have it—dried herbs, even a bay leaf in a dish. Worst case? Just speak aloud your offering. Smoke helps, but your words carry weight.

Dog ate your flowers?

Yeah. That happened. Offer a silent laugh to Lakshmi and place a fresh flower when you can. Spirits love humor as much as beauty.

You got interrupted mid-prayer?

Finish what you can. Then pause, close your eyes, and say, "I return now to complete this." Pick it back up when things settle.

You're feeling disconnected or flat?

It happens. Sit. Breathe. Say her name softly. Don't force it. Just show up and keep showing up. The connection deepens over time.

You started with great energy, then forgot about the whole thing?

This one's common. Ritual builds momentum. When you break that, energy fades. Don't beat yourself up. Recommit.

Even one flame can restart the current.

Want to fix almost any ritual problem?

Say this: "Lakshmi, I return now. I reset this working with love, clarity, and devotion."

That's it. Rituals bend for you—not the other way around.

Ten Names of Lakshmi (With Meanings)

1. Sri Lakshmi

The radiant and benevolent one. The full embodiment of wealth, grace, and divine beauty.

2. Mahalakshmi

The Great Lakshmi. The supreme goddess of abundance, power, and spiritual liberation.

3. Padma Lakshmi

Lakshmi of the Lotus. Symbol of purity, detachment, and spiritual blossoming. She rises untouched, even from the mud.

4. Dhana Lakshmi

Goddess of material wealth. Bringer of gold, coins, property, and financial blessings.

5. Dhanya Lakshmi

Goddess of agricultural wealth. Feeds the family, blesses the harvest, and ensures nourishment.

6. Gaja Lakshmi

Lakshmi of power and royalty. She restores wealth, status, and honor. Usually flanked by elephants.

7. Santana Lakshmi

Goddess of fertility, lineage, and healthy children. Bringer of legacy and generational growth.

8. Veera Lakshmi

Lakshmi of courage and strength. Grants inner power, endurance, and victory in hard times.

9. Vijaya Lakshmi

Lakshmi of success and triumph. Helps overcome obstacles and win battles—physical, financial, or spiritual.

10. Aishwarya Lakshmi

Lakshmi of divine opulence. Grants luxury, recognition, and elevated status in the world.

You can call each of these by name or chant them like a mantra. Example: "Padma Lakshmi, bless me with clarity and grace." Keep it personal. She responds to devotion, not recitation.

Power Affirmations to Speak Daily

Here's a clean, tight set of Lakshmi-aligned Power Affirmations—designed to hit all the key flows: wealth, love, harmony, and destiny. Speak them out loud. Whisper them. Write them. Doesn't matter—just mean them.

Wealth

"I am aligned with divine wealth. Money flows to me with

ease."

"Abundance surrounds me and fills my life daily."

"I welcome sudden windfalls and steady streams of income."

Love

"I radiate love and receive it in return."

"My relationships are filled with joy, honesty, and deep connection."

"I attract partners, allies, and friends who see my true worth."

Harmony

"Peace lives in my home, my body, and my thoughts."

"Every room I enter fills with harmony and warmth."

"I move through the day with grace and calm."

Destiny

"I walk the path meant for me. All doors open at the right time."

"Lakshmi guides my steps. I trust the timing of my life."

"My destiny is abundance in all forms—spiritual, emotional, and material."

Use these however you like:

During morning ritual, before bed, while staring into a candle, or in the car on a bad day. You're not begging. You're affirming alignment. That's how this works.

The Path to Lakshmi

This symbolic map walks you through the energetic journey toward Lakshmi's presence. Each step is a stage of alignment.

You start with the offering—flowers, incense, a whisper of intention. That's the first gate.

Next comes the candle—your will, igniting. This is the moment you say yes to her energy. The fire sends the signal.

Then the mantra spiral, spoken or internal, begins spinning your field into harmony. Each repetition tightens the thread between your world and hers.

The yantra center focuses the connection. Here's where the energy condenses. You visualize. You feel. You land.

Finally, you reach Lakshmi on the lotus, seated in radiance. She's above the noise. You've climbed the current, shifted your frequency, and stepped into the flow.

This isn't just an image. It's a visual spell.

Use it like a map. Trace it with your eyes. Walk it in meditation.

Let it become muscle memory.

She will meet you there.

THE PATH TO LAKSHMI

Yantras

(Full color versions available at:
https://davepsychic.com/lakshmi-book-yantras/)

SRI YANTRA

HEART HARMONY YANTRA

MONEY-FLOW YANTRA

RTA ALIGNMENT YANTRA

SEVEN-GATE SPIRAL

GLOSSARY

Key Terms (Alphabetical)

Abhishekam

A ritual bath offered to a deity's image. You pour milk, water, honey, or rosewater over the statue while chanting. It's not about washing—it's a full-bodied offering of devotion.

Alakshmi

The shadow of Lakshmi. She brings poverty, discord, and chaos when you act with greed, ego, or dishonor. She's not evil—she's the balancing force.

Aarti

A short fire ritual, done at the end of a puja. You circle the flame in front of the deity as a way of sealing the moment with light.

Anahata

The heart chakra. Where divine love, clarity, and emotional wealth flow. Lakshmi energy loves to settle here. When this is blocked, everything else feels off.

Bhupura

The outer square boundary of a yantra. Symbolizes the threshold between ordinary space and sacred space. The gate where you step into focus.

Bindu

The center point of a yantra. All creation spirals from it. Meditating here brings you into direct contact with the divine pattern.

Dharma

Your soul's path. Not a job—your actual alignment. Lakshmi responds when you're walking in it. If you're not, expect turbulence.

Drishti

Your internal or external gaze. Where you look, energy flows. It's crucial in visualization, ritual, and manifestation.

Grihalakshmi

Lakshmi in her role as the guardian of the home. She governs peace, harmony, food, family flow, and domestic wealth.

Lakshmi

The central goddess of this book. Divine source of wealth, love, beauty, spiritual clarity, and prosperity. She brings what you're ready for.

Loka

A plane of existence. Earth is one. Lakshmi's subtle zone is another. You can travel between lokas in meditation, pathworking, or death.

Mala

A string of 108 beads. Used for mantra repetition. Helps focus your mind while embedding the sound code into your field.

Mantra

A sacred sound or phrase. Chanted to invoke Lakshmi's energy and realign your frequency. Not affirmations—vibrational commands.

Mudra

A hand gesture used to activate energy flows. Every finger position holds meaning. These are subtle switches in your body's circuit.

Nadis

The energy channels that run through your subtle body. Blocked nadis mean stalled progress. Open ones mean energy flows freely.

Puja

A ritual of offering and invocation. Could be one candle or a full altar. What matters is presence, intent, and sincerity.

Prasad

The offering you give during ritual—returned to you, now blessed. Often food, but not always. You're taking the goddess into yourself.

Rta (Ṛta)

The cosmic law. The natural order. When you align with Rta, everything flows. Violate it, and life kicks back hard.

Sankalpa

Your stated intention before a ritual. Said aloud, calmly, and with focus. You're locking in your target frequency.

Sattva

The energy of clarity, calm, and balance. This is the best state for spiritual work. Clean space, clean heart, steady mind.

Shakti

Divine feminine power. Raw, moving life force. Lakshmi is a face of Shakti. When she stirs, reality bends around her.

Tarpana

An ancestral offering. Done to clear old karma, honor your roots, and stop wealth blocks from your bloodline.

Yantra

A sacred diagram. Printed geometry that works like a spell. Focus on it, and you access the spirit encoded inside.

About The Author

Dave is an author of adult fantasy (The Furies series) as well as author of occult books about magick. Dave has multiple advanced degrees in the occult, including a Doctorate in Literature, plus Doctor Honoris causa in Ancient Religions, Doctor Honoris causa in Demonology, Doctor Honoris causa in Divinity, Doctor Honoris causa in Magik.

He began working ritual magik back in the 1970s. He took a brief break, then used the power of this magik to create a photography career which took him to Los Angeles and work as a photographer for multiple magazines.

Dave has studied magik in all forms, and in 2018, released a three-part magik instruction course in High Magik. Thousands of students have benefited from David's unique teaching style, making ceremonial magik accessible to everyone.

Dave also has a series on Grecian Magick, exploring the aspects of ceremonial magick with the gods and goddesses of ancient Greece.

Magik Books by David Thompson
Available as EPUB, Paperback and Hardcover ()

High Magick Series
- High Magick 101
- Daemons of High Magick
- Daemons and the Law of Attraction
- Magick of Astaroth
- Hidden in Plain Sight
- Lilith: Goddess of Darkness and Light
- Daemons of Fortune
- Asmodeus King of Daemons
- Goddesses of High Magick
- Protection Magik
- The Diviner's Handbook
- The Magik of Lucifer
- The Magik of Freya and Frigg
- The Magik of Sorath
- Goddesses of Vengeance
- Magik of Genius Spirits
- Power of Pathworking

Norse Magik

- Odin and Thor

Hindu Magik
- Magik of Lakshmi

Grecian Magick Series
- Magick of Apollo
- Magick of Hermes
- Magick of Aphrodite
- Magick of Fortuna
- Greco-Roman Wealth Magick
- Magick of the Sirens/Magick of the Muses
- Hermes and the Akashic Records

Magik for Everyone Series
- Candle Magik for Everyone
- Magik of Love & Lust

Fiction Novels by David Thompson

The Furies Series
- Angels of Vengeance
- Descent into Tartarus
- Furies: Beginnings
- Brianna: Making of a Fury

To connect with Dave, you can check his website at

https://davepsychic.com

Social media links are at https://davepsychic.com/social-media-links/

www.ingramcontent.com/pod-product-compliance
Lightning Source LLC
Chambersburg PA
CBHW071401120626
46546CB00002B/771